THE LIVES & LOVES OF THE DELAMERES

Vale Royal, White Mischief and the Delves Broughtons

R.M.Bevan

Published in 2021
by C.C.Publishing
(Chester)

ISBN
978-0-949001-67-2

C.C. PUBLISHING, MARTINS LANE, HARGRAVE, CHESTER, CH3 7RX
TEL: 01829 741651. EMAIL: editor@cc-publishing.co.uk
WEBSITE: http://www.cc-publishing.co.uk

Cover photograph: Phyllis Lady Delamere.

Contents

Preface

VALE Royal Abbey is the most beguiling and yet probably the least known historic setting in Cheshire. The place has fascinated me for over sixty years, a boyhood adventure to wander Sandiway golf course and sneak into the forbidden and forbidding precincts. Embellished in their telling we had heard the blood-curdling tales of ghosts and headless monks and at the faintest of shadow, or echo on timeworn cobbles, we were off, not stopping until we had passed the grinning stone carvings of Monkey Lodge.

Later, as a reporter and then editor of the local *Northwich Guardian,* I penned many an article about the uncertain fate of Vale Royal, centuries of history, its very survival often hanging by no more than a gossamer thread. Stories engrained in folklore, the mightiest monastery of England endowed by one king and razed to the ground by another.

Then came generations of the Delameres, an ancient landed family rooted in Cheshire since William the Conqueror. The most remarkable of them all was the 3rd Baron Delamere. Small in stature and yet a mountainous figure he sacrificed Vale Royal to shape and found a nation and a dynasty thousands of miles away.

Now largely forgotten in his native land and denounced in his adopted country, he left a legacy that would become

Kenya, the backdrop to one of the most enduring murder mysteries of all time, its impact felt nowhere greater than in Cheshire. It is specifically from the Cheshire perspective that I have brought together this account focused on Vale Royal, the Delameres and their neighbours and friends, the Delves Broughtons, a family ensnared in notoriety due to the 11th Baronet and his wife, a scarlet woman who went on to become the eighth Lady Delamere of Vale Royal.

Finally there are astonishing recent events surrounding the tragedy of the 3rd Baron Delamere's great-grandson who twice escaped the gallows charged with murder in Kenya.

On the subject of Kenya, it is important within context to briefly understand its evolution: From 1895 to 1920 the country was a British protectorate known as East Africa. It became Kenya Colony in 1920 and upon full independence, in 1964, the modern Republic of Kenya.

I wish to acknowledge three outstanding books I have particularly used for source material, Elspeth Huxley's two-volume work *White Man's Country*; James Fox's *White Mischief*; and Leda Farrant's *Diana, Lady Delamere, and the Lord Erroll Murder.*

R.M.Bevan

1

A King's solemn vow

HAUNTINGS, legends and mysteries have swirled in the river mists of Vale Royal Abbey for a thousand years. Kings have tarried here, a Ploughboy Prophet has told of great events and ghostly figures are said to appear in the half-moonlight – a headless monk, a veiled lady, apparitions flitting across darkened windows, celestial music drifting on the cold night air. Far removed from the supernatural and superstition there are other ghosts and these stand silent testimony to the Lives and Loves of an extraordinary Cheshire family, the birth of an African nation and one of the 20th century's most sensational unsolved murders.

Vale Royal sits in the village of Whitegate at the heart of rolling countryside, fifteen miles from the county town of Chester and almost four thousand from Kenya and the one-time stamping ground of the notorious Happy Valley set, a small, hedonistic cabal of largely British expatriates lorded over by predatory womaniser Josslyn Victor Hay, the 22nd Earl of Erroll, who, at the height of the Second World War, was found dead on a lonely road near Nairobi. He had been shot in the head and so was born an enigma that has intrigued investigators and writers for eighty years. Books by the dozen have been penned and widely varying theories abound from a lovers' tiff, cuckolded husbands, jilted lovers, conspiracy and even assassination by the British secret service.

One of the best of these tomes – not quite the first, but certainly the most riveting – is James Fox's *White Mischief*, forerunner of a blockbuster film starring Greta Scacchi and Charles Dance. Fox wrote his book after assisting a *Sunday Times*' colleague, Cyril

Connolly, on a meticulous search for the truth behind the Earl of Erroll's death and what they unearthed stirred up steamy emotions and controversy in both England and Kenya.

Born in Washington, the son of an American international lawyer and an English mother, Fox cut his teeth as an investigative reporter on the *Manchester Evening News*, many of his early assignments conducted in Cheshire, and whilst investigating the Erroll mystery he became fascinated that such a notorious murder, half a world away, had its roots so deeply embedded in the county's fertile soil.

"Cheshire is perhaps the real heartland of the landowning classes," he said. "It's the richest part of the country, has the finest hunting, the glossiest horses, and so on. Maybe Cheshire is a place apart. I wonder if there is something particularly feudal about Cheshire? The most feudal characters most certainly got on well in Kenya." Indeed, Kenya was stuffed with Cheshire names and one that continues to resonate above all others is Delamere, i.e. the Delameres originally of Vale Royal, the "Kennedys of Kenya" who, similar to their American counterparts, have so often found themselves mired in scandal. The English ancestry of the Delameres, or to give them their family name "Cholmondeley", traces all the way back to a half-blood nephew of William the Conqueror and for centuries they sat at Cheshire's top table with the likes of the Breretons, Duttons, Egertons, Grosvenors and Vernons etc – James Fox's feudal landlords, men of great estates possessed of immense power and prestige.

Others of this elite circle were the Delves Broughtons who, for hundreds of years, maintained one foot in Cheshire and one in Staffordshire. The Delves Broughtons' ancient family home, forty minutes' drive from Vale Royal, was, and still is, Doddington Park on the old London Road out of Nantwich, and from here the 11th

Vale Royal Abbey. Stonework and timber from the abbey was used to build the mansion

Baronet, Sir Henry John (Jock) Delves Broughton, stood trial for his life in Kenya, charged with the murder of the Earl of Erroll.

Vale Royal Abbey, from which grew the country house mansion of the Delameres, was personally founded in the 13th century by no less than King Edward I who, fanciful legend has it, escaped shipwreck whilst returning from the Holy Lands and, consequently, made a solemn vow to the blessed Virgin Mary that he would build in his kingdom a monastery unparalleled in "liberties, wealth and honour throughout the whole world".

He chose for his site a small Saxon settlement in a remote wooded river valley alongside Cheshire's ancient forest of Delamere. And so, in August 1277, accompanied by Queen Eleanor and a Plantagenet assemblage of lords, barons and bishops from every corner of the realm, he laid the foundation stone of what was to become the mighty Cistercian abbey of Vallis Regalis, one of the largest works of piety ever commissioned by a medieval English monarch. A colossal undertaking, plagued by civil wars, political upheaval and financial difficulties, it took over fifty years to construct Vale Royal and, though much work was still required, a grand feast took place in 1330 to mark the new abbey's dedication. Naturally, the occasion was touched by the Hand of God as, for almost forty days and forty nights floods of Noah's Ark proportions struck the district until, miraculously, on the big day "not a drop of water fell upon the earth".

The Cistercians built over ninety monasteries in Britain, their rules stipulating these were to be erected in places remote from the "conversation of men" and Vale Royal, with Combermere, Stanlow and Poulton, was one of four in Cheshire. However, none in the entire kingdom was more extensively favoured by ruling monarchs and royal charter than Vale Royal. Constructed at enormous cost, incorporating a crowning glory of

Stained-glass window from Vale Royal Abbey, now in the Burrell Museum, Glasgow, depicts King Edward. It was in the interests of successive abbots to perpetuate the myth of divine intervention, that Vale Royal was preordained by God.

twelve chapels, it briefly dwarfed Westminster Abbey and all of the Cistercian abbeys, including Fountains, Tintern and Furness. That was until 1360 when a ferocious storm brought down the nave, its massive stone collars "like trees uprooted by the wind" and, with Royal blessing, the giant structure had to be scaled down in size. In terms of wealth, the abbey never recovered from the disaster, regardless of the best business efforts of hard-nosed abbots skilled in theology, the collection of tithes and exploitation of the peasantry.

What King Edward I began in 1277, King Henry VIII finished during the English Reformation when his fixer-in-chief, Thomas Cromwell, arrived to preside over a special court to determine the abbey's fate and, amidst accusations of treason and murder, the white-robed Cistercian monks were abruptly expelled. Not that King Henry would have concerned himself with Vale Royal, or the legal blather. He was far too busy chopping off heads and chasing wifely conquests – Ann Boleyn beheaded 1536, Jane Seymour married 1536, Anne of Cleves 1540, Catherine Howard 1540, Catherine Parr 1543. And so at the height of His Majesty's madness, Vale Royal Abbey was handed over to a royal commissioner, Sir Thomas Holcroft, who quickly reported he had "plucked the place down" and a thorough job he made of it. Not a visible stone from the abbey church was left standing and, consequently, there are no ruins of national monument status to remind of those turbulent times when Vale Royal Abbey towered head and shoulders above the likes of Westminster, Fountains, Tintern and Furness.

Sir Thomas Holcroft, courtier and politician, rose to prominence on the patronage of Thomas Cromwell and together they seem to have been engaged in nod-and-wink land speculation. Never one to miss an opportunity to expand his portfolio, Holcroft paid the King £450 to purchase Vale Royal with its monastic estate and, immediately, he set about utilising the stonework and timber from the abbey ruins to build himself a mansion alongside the sacred site, his design apparently incorporating the cloisters and some of the domestic buildings. A circular stone monument, erected much later by the Delameres, is believed to mark the original High Altar and this became the inspiration for a local solicitor, John Henry Cooke, to write his acclaimed romantic novel *Ida – the Mystery of the Nun's Grave.*

As it turned out, the Holcroft family's occupation was relatively short-lived and, at the start of the 17th century, Vale Royal house and its monastic estate, including land originally carved from Delamere Forest, was sold to Lady Mary Cholmondeley, a formidable Tudor aristocrat who stood her ground for women's rights centuries before Emmeline Pankhurst and the Suffragettes. Much of Lady Mary's eventful life was engaged in lawsuits she fought with sustained determination, especially a forty years' battle to inherit her father's estate on the outskirts of the town of Northwich. Energetic, courageous and independent, Lady Mary purchased Vale Royal and numerous other properties following the death of her husband, Sir Hugh Cholmondeley. They had eight children, two sons succeeding to the family's primary estate centred on Cholmondeley Castle, another inheriting Vale Royal, and one of the daughters marrying into the Grosvenors.

The Dolgellau Chalice and Plate supposedly made at the command of King Edward for Vale Royal Abbey. Crafted from the captured gold of Welsh princes these were later stolen and lay hidden near Dolgellau until 1890. Now displayed in The National Museum of Wales.

2

Tragedy and Scandal

LADY Mary Cholmondeley was the first of many remarkable chatelaines associated with Vale Royal and when King James I held court here whilst hunting stag in Delamere Forest, he dubbed her the "Bolde Ladie of Cheshyre". A deserved epithet, her indomitable spirit was to shine through succeeding generations and in 1821, to mark the coronation of King George IV, one of her descendants, Thomas Cholmondeley, took the family to new heights when he was raised to the peerage as Baron Delamere, a reward for his purse rather than personal or political achievement.

Thomas had to pay an enormous price for the privilege as the present 5th Lord Delamere has noted: "My great-great-grandfather bought the title from the Duke of Wellington. He was an idiot who decided it would be impressive to have a peerage. He thought he had a bargain when he paid £5,000 for it. The only problem was that the going rate was £1,200. Before he came along we had been content to be shire knights in Cheshire, when William the Conqueror gave us the whole county." [1]

Money is a recurring theme in the story of the Delameres and regardless of whether or not Thomas the 1st Baron, Member of Parliament and High Sheriff of Cheshire, paid over the odds for his peerage, he and his wife Henrietta lavishly overspent for thirty

1. The title "Baron Delamere" can be confusing. The family has never owned the forest of Delamere. This has always been held by the Earl of Chester and latterly the Crown. When King Edward I founded Vale Royal he included in his granting of the monastic estate a part of the forest's extreme eastern boundary (Weaverham, Sandiway, Over etc). This passed to Lady Mary Cholmondeley when she purchased Vale Royal from Sir Thomas Holcroft early in the 17th century.

Thomas Cholmondeley, the 1st Baron (Lord) Delamere.

years, beautifying the great house, adding priceless antiques and works of art, and modernising the estate with new farmhouses, cottages and lodges. It was a far cry from Thomas's grandfather who had been forced to sell thousands of acres of land to settle heavy debts incurred in foolishly trying to establish an iron foundry on the estate with Coalbrookdale's Abraham Darby. Indeed, at every second generation, custodians of Vale Royal seem to have trended from one extravagant hairbrained scheme to another, and without basic raw materials the iron foundry was an early investment folly.

The 1st Lady Delamere, Thomas's wife Henrietta, was one of eight children to North Wales' richest and most powerful landowner Sir Watkin Williams-Wynn whose wife, Lady Charlotte Grenville, was a daughter of former British Prime Minister George Grenville. The Delameres were not in the same rich league as the Williams-Wynns and, more than likely, it was Sir Watkin who dubbed up the

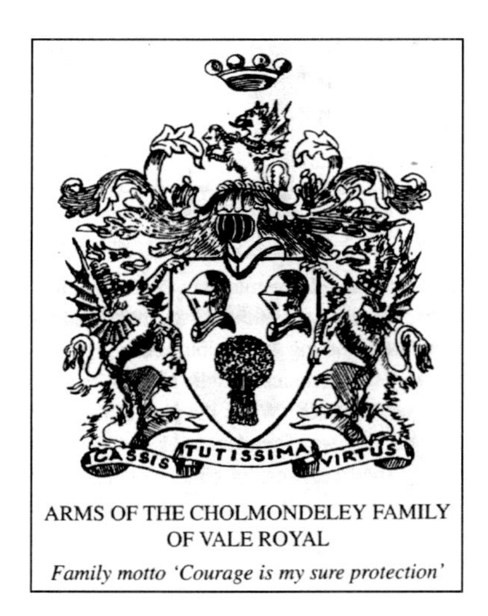

ARMS OF THE CHOLMONDELEY FAMILY OF VALE ROYAL
Family motto 'Courage is my sure protection'

£5,000 to elevate his daughter to the exalted position as the wife of an English peer. Also helpful was Henrietta's political connection through her grandfather George Grenville and as Lady Delamere she and her husband entertained lavishly at their London town-house, their circle of socialite friends including such Regency notables as the dandy Beau Brummell and the poet, politician Lord Byron. Once said to be "mad, bad and dangerous to know" as far as women were concerned, Byron struck up a close relationship with Henrietta who, allegedly, invited him to spend five days at Vale Royal whilst her husband was absent on Parliamentary duty in London. What took place we shall never know, but Byron apparently presented Henrietta with a hand-written, signed copy of his latest poem, "She Walks in Beauty", and for many years the document was prominently displayed, with other valuable books and manuscripts, in a glass case at Vale Royal.

Hugh, the 2nd Baron Delamere.

When Hugh, the 2nd Baron Delamere, inherited in 1855 he found the Vale Royal coffers seriously depleted and yet, in marked contrast to his father before him and his son to follow, he proved a far more compassionate and approachable protector of the estate. A retired officer with the Life Guards, a colonel with the Cheshire Militia and a former

The 2nd Baron and Lady Augusta.

Member of Parliament for Denbighshire and Montgomery, the 2nd Baron was wracked by tragedy when his wife of twelve years, Lady Sarah Hay-Drummond, the 2nd Lady Delamere, died at the age of thirty-one. Bound up in the mists of Scottish history, Lady Sarah's father was the 11th Earl of Kinnoull who shared a common ancestry with the Earls of Erroll, the Hereditary Lord High Constables of Scotland, ironically a family with whom Vale Royal and the Delameres would become inextricably entwined in 20th century Kenya. The Earl of Kinnoull's other titles included Lord Hay of Kifauns and Baron Hay of Penwardine.

Lonely and devastated by Lady Sarah's death, Hugh did not mourn for long and within a year he married Augusta Emily

Seymour, a feisty, headstrong and hot-tempered young woman. Their marriage was never close and Lady Augusta, the 3rd Lady Delamere, confessed she hated Vale Royal and found Cheshire "the most boring place to live".

Her father, a leading British diplomat, is said to have presented Hugh with a solid gold snuff box for taking his precocious daughter off his hands and though, perhaps, an over-exaggerated tale this reinforces what most villagers came to think of Lady Augusta, severe and cantankerous. Incidentally, the gold snuff box was one of scores of precious items disposed of by later Vale Royal generations. It is currently owned by a resident of Saudi Arabia.

Lord Delamere did his best to make Vale Royal more appealing and in preparation for their wedding, in December 1860, he embarked on further costly improvements to the house. Not that Lady Augusta was impressed and she may well have quoted Alexander Pope's lines:

I find by all you have been talking
That 'tis a house, but not a dwelling.

To make matters worse, Lord Delamere then insensitively commissioned the building of St John's Church and school, in the then village of Over, as a permanent memorial to his first wife, Lady Sarah. The project cost him dearly, £5,000 he could ill afford, and Lady Augusta, antagonised by what she must have considered a crass faux pas, never showed any inkling to settle at Vale Royal. She much preferred to live and socialise in Bournemouth, or at their Bruton Street, London home, and for years until her husband's death she flitted in and out of Vale Royal, staff and villagers ever wary of her lashing tongue and tantrums. And if that wasn't enough she further infuriated the locals by bringing about closure of their sole public house, the Rifleman (now Whitegate House), because of what she termed "unseemly behaviour" on the village green.

Eventually, Lady Augusta fell pregnant in London, but the child was stillborn and, to further strain their marriage, rumours abounded that Lord Delamere was having an affair with his housekeeper at Vale Royal. Not to be outdone, Lady Augusta finally bore him a son and heir, the 3rd Baron Delamere, explorer and nation builder, and also a daughter, Sybil. Although rather than dampening her husband's ardour, he returned to Vale Royal and fathered two illegitimate sons with the housekeeper. In his will, and presumably by way of gratitude as much as duty, he left Lady Augusta well provided for, bequeathing her property, horses, carriages, jewellery and £1,000 a year.

St John's Church, Over (John Mears Collection).

3

Temper of the Devil

WHEN they buried the 2nd Lord Delamere at Whitegate Church there were few mourners who did not contemplate what the future might hold for the Vale Royal estate and its tenants. Succession was passing to a wayward seventeen-year-old who had scant regard for Victorian convention, or the lineage of his forebears, but none on that solemn September day in 1887 could possibly have foreseen that this rather insignificant young man, small with ginger hair, large nose and piercing blue eyes, was destined to indelibly etch his name in a faraway country.

Born on April 28, 1870 at his parents' London residence in Mayfair, Hugh Cholmondeley was inheriting a title and a hunting stable though, frustratingly for one with such an impetuous nature, he would have to wait until his twenty-fifth birthday in order to gain control of the estate's governing trust amounting to £49,000 in his father's will. Contradictory, opinionated and unpredictable, Hugh, always known informally as Hughie, could be good company and charming when the mood took him but, intrinsically, he was a rebel, a young man forever seeking his next thrill and, possessed with the temper of the devil, an obvious trait inherited from his mother's genes, woe betide anyone who crossed him.

Much of Hugh's early life was spent away from Vale Royal in the company of his mother, sister and a governess whom he terrorised. He never got on with his aged father, seventy-five on his death, and there was always a chasm between them. Indeed, the 2nd Baron took such scant interest in his son's upbringing that Lady Augusta was prompted to describe her husband as a "weak person without

The 2nd Lord Delamere's funeral at Whitegate in 1887.

strength of character". Inevitably young Hugh took his mother's side – the emotional scars associated with his father's illegitimate children and the money siphoned from the estate to build St John's Church remained festering sores until the end.

Young Hugh Delamere, the 3rd Baron.

For all that, and whilst attending boarding school in Winchester, Hugh looked forward to holidays at Vale Royal when the family would briefly reunite. Full of boyish pranks, his playground was the countryside, the banks of the River Weaver and the great rambling house with miles of corridors, its centrepiece great hall (saloon) adorned with heraldic shields and coronets of his ancestors, and King James' preserved oak-panelled bedchamber where Hugh took great delight in spooking the housemaids. Another of his oft-performed daredevil pranks, to scare the living daylights out of outdoor workers, was to ride his bicycle full pelt towards a brick wall and then jump off at the very last second. The older he got the more mischievous he became and in the middle of one unforgettable night he even stole into Whitegate Church and, for the sheer hell of it, rang the bells to raise villagers from their slumbers.

Old houses have their legends and few are older and more mysterious than Vale Royal. When Hugh was growing up he must have heard them all – the ghostly story of a 14th century nun wandering the grounds, an abbot in search of his head, plundering Civil War Parliamentarians and, above all, the tales of Prophet Nixon, Cheshire's own Mother Shipton. Born and raised on the estate, the old seer's sayings and prophecies, legends that seemed to reside in the space between fact and fiction, were taken seriously in these parts and, for as long as anyone could remember, an eagle was kept at Vale Royal because he had foretold that the birth of a son and heir depended on it. Perhaps, more ominously, Nixon also predicted that if rocks from Warrington were ever to "visit" Vale Royal then the sun would set on the ancient family and, not too many years before Hugh's birth, superstitious locals wondered when a viaduct was built through the abbey grounds to carry the Grand Junction Railway. It was constructed of Warrington sandstone!

The brooding weight of ancestry rested on Hugh's shoulders and, to remind him, portraits of illustrious forebears gazed down at every turn. The most notable of these was his great-great grandfather, Thomas Pitt, sporting in his cocked hat a diamond as "big as a plum". This was the so-called "Pitt Diamond", a 141-carat perfect brilliant Thomas had rather dubiously acquired whilst serving as a British governor in India. Later he sold the gem, as large as the Koh-i-Noor Diamond, to the Duke of Orleans for the sum of £135,000, though it's questionable if this astonishing amount was ever paid. "Le Regent", as it came to be known in France, was worn by Louis XV, decorated Marie Antoinette's hat and embellished Napoleon's coronation sword. Now one of the crown jewels of France, it has been on permanent display at the Louvre since 1887 and is valued at over £50 million.

The Pitt Diamond.

Records in Cheshire reveal that from the original cutting

A portrait of Thomas Pitt with the diamond hung at Vale Royal for two centuries.

process, Thomas Pitt also sold fragments to Peter the Great of Russia and from what remained he had a necklace crafted for his daughter, Essex Pitt, who had married into the Vale Royal family in 1714. It is through Essex Pitt that the Delameres come to have in their family tree the British Prime Ministers William Pitt the Elder and William Pitt the Younger, as well as the previously mentioned George Grenville.

However the Delameres were not, as asserted by numerous writers and websites, directly related to Sir Robert Walpole, Britain's first Prime Minister. The confusion seems to have arisen because, in 1723, one of Walpole's daughters married into the Cholmondeley Castle family, although by then the Vale Royal branch had been independently established for over a century.

At thirteen, Hugh Delamere had other matters on his mind as he took his place at Eton to follow the traditional route of most sons of the ruling class. Unfortunately, he lacked scholarly ambition and the cloistered environment merely served to increase his wilfulness. Trouble followed him and, if it didn't, he went looking for it as when he wrecked a boot-shop in Windsor High Street and then bunked off to attend Ascot races, the latter a misdemeanor for which he was severely flogged. Hugh intensely disliked Eton and the public school luminaries were, no doubt, glad to see the back of him when, at the age of seventeen, he was allowed to opt out, ostensibly to pursue a career in the Life Guards, his father's old regiment, although as it turned out his military prowess did not advance beyond the rank of captain in the Cheshire Yeomanry Cavalry.

Believed to be Essex Pitt whose name has run through generations of the family. Her nephew was William Pitt the Elder, her great nephew William Pitt the Younger.

The 2nd Baron's unexpected death of course changed the landscape and though Hugh looked on the great house as akin to a mausoleum he briefly settled with his mother at Vale Royal and she was soon pressing on him the importance of participating in the London season and marrying a well-heeled daughter of the nobility whose dowry would assure the future of the family and the estate. However, Hugh had no time for such niceties, or convention for that matter, and rather than tempering his unruliness, Lady Augusta only succeeded in fuelling his dreams of overseas' travel and big-game hunting in Africa. As a compromise he was permitted to visit Corsica and in the following year even managed to persuade his mother to accompany him to New Zealand, a trip, as far as he was concerned, that could not have worked out better. New Zealand did not appeal to Lady Augusta and she soon returned to England, leaving Hugh to find his way to an Australian squatters' station where he stayed for several months and picked up the rudiments of sheep farming. It was to be a life-changing experience.

Vale Royal Abbey.

Whitegate Church and Lodge.

Monkey Lodge at the entrance to New Park.

The Abbey Arms, Oakmere, and the Blue Cap,
Sandiway, were part of the Vale Royal Estate.

Grenville Lodge, at the Hartford entrance to Vale
Royal, was named after the 1st Lady Delamere's
Prime Minister grandfather. Now demolished
it was also known as Grosvenor Lodge.

4
Man of Destiny

HUGH Delamere came of age in 1891 and, following in the footsteps of his grandfather, he was elected the youngest member of the Tarporley Hunt Club, the most exclusive and oldest hunt club in England. Membership was by invitation only, open to prominent landed gentry who owned most of the county, and since 1762 the first week in November had been set aside for hunting and feasting, when the red carpet would be rolled out at Cheshire's own House of Lords, Tarporley's Swan Hotel, where the presidential crests and names adorned the walls like pages of history.

As plump as partridges, green-collared and red-coated, partaking of a veritable feast and chatting about their grand estates, these feudal landlords still floated on a glittering sea of never-ending privilege and prosperity, but it was a gilded age hurtling towards closure, under attack from the common legions of industrialisation sweeping inexorably towards their isolated pastures. And, more than anywhere, the future looked uncertain for Vale Royal pincered incongruously between the expanding Northwich and Winsford hell-holes of salt and chemical production.

Hugh Delamere loved hunting and for a couple of years he threw himself into the spirit and camaraderie of the Tarporley Hunt Club, especially the intriguingly named "Bachelor Ordinaries" whereby every Saturday after a hard day's hunting, a bachelor member would throw a rowdy dinner and gambling party at his home. Ladies were excluded and only the occasional married man was invited as a special compliment. Horseracing was another magnet and frequenting the many local courses Hugh gambled heavily

The Tarporley Hunt Club based at The Swan since 1762.

which was hardly surprising as the Duke of Westminster, a senior member of the Hunt Club, was the owner of four Derby winners and, for well over a century, the district around Tarporley was regarded as one of the North of England's most important training centres.

Free at last to please himself, Hugh switched his attention to pursuing his long-held big-game hunting ambition, although his first two trips could not have been more of a contrast, India and Norway, both of which succeeded only in further slaking his thirst for excitement in Africa, the last great unexplored continent.

And so Hugh embarked on an expedition to British Somaliland where he became so hooked he returned, year after year, and would send back to Vale Royal a vast array of "trophies" which were later described by his agent's daughter: "There were full-sized lions made to look as if they were fighting; elephants' heads, leopard skins and rhinos. One elephant's foot had been hollowed out to hold bottles of whisky and gin and a cigar box. Many of these trophies were later sent to the Liverpool Museum which was destroyed in the blitz of the Second World War."

Hugh also contributed articles to a national magazine and, as a result, was universally hailed as the "greatest and most plucky game hunter of the century", although of course it came at a price. His expeditions were hugely expensive and, not a rich man by upper class standards of the day, he was forced to borrow £27,000 to finance his extravagant lifestyle and, predictably, receivers were appointed to collect the Vale Royal estate's meagre income on behalf of his mortgagees. Even so, he still managed to lose £3,000 on a single bet at Chester Races.

He was living beyond his means and in 1895 he endorsed the receivers' intention to raise additional income by letting out the house and park as, after all, he was seldom in residence and his mother had, more or less, retreated to her home in Bournemouth. Unfortunately the following advertisement in *The Field* magazine attracted little interest:

> Vale Royal, Cheshire (the beautiful home of a nobleman). To let for a term of years. Exquisitely furnished. Stands in a large well-timbered park, and contains a fine suite of reception rooms, including magnificent saloon and library, billiard room, twenty principal bed and dressing rooms, sixteen servants' bedrooms, bathroom, lavatories. There is very good stabling for twenty horses, two large coach houses, also dairy, laundry and several cottages together with about 50 acres of grassland. Shooting over about 700 acres, fishing in the lakes in the park. Strongly recommended.

On top of financial problems Hugh was never in the most robust of health, although he did possess remarkable powers of endurance and these came to the fore during his third trip to Somaliland when he contracted typhoid fever and, later, was badly mauled by a lion. The shock alone would have killed most men and afterwards he reckoned he owed his life to the fact that for five days he lay absolutely still on his back where he had fallen. Somali gun bearers built a little shelter over him and, twice a day, he used a penknife to lance his black and festering ankle wound so the poison would drain away. For the rest of his life he walked with a slight limp.

Such a brush with death would have put off most men, but not Hugh Delamere, and he was more determined than ever to explore the East African wilderness. In 1897 at the zenith of Britain's imperial glory, when the rest of Britain was preparing to celebrate Queen Victoria's Diamond Jubilee, he set out at the head of an expedition to cross the deserts of south Somaliland into largely uncharted British East Africa. Further impoverishing the Vale Royal estate, he financed the entire shooting match, his caravan train made up of two hundred camels, one-hundred guards and bearers, doctor, taxidermist and photographer. Following a route previously taken by only four white men, Hugh and his party trekked for a thousand miles until they came upon a vast area of untouched, lush highlands and cedar-forested slopes, a temperate patch of Africa in the lowland folds of Mount Kenya. Here the altitude made the climate cooler and moister and he saw the finest pastures of his homeland in a perpetual English summer. The possibilities enraptured him and, from that moment, the long-term fate of Vale Royal was sealed.

His mother, Lady Augusta, had not seen him for eighteen months and she must have been at her wit's end when, with his whereabouts unknown, British newspapers speculated that he had been killed by natives. Fortunately it was an unfounded rumour and

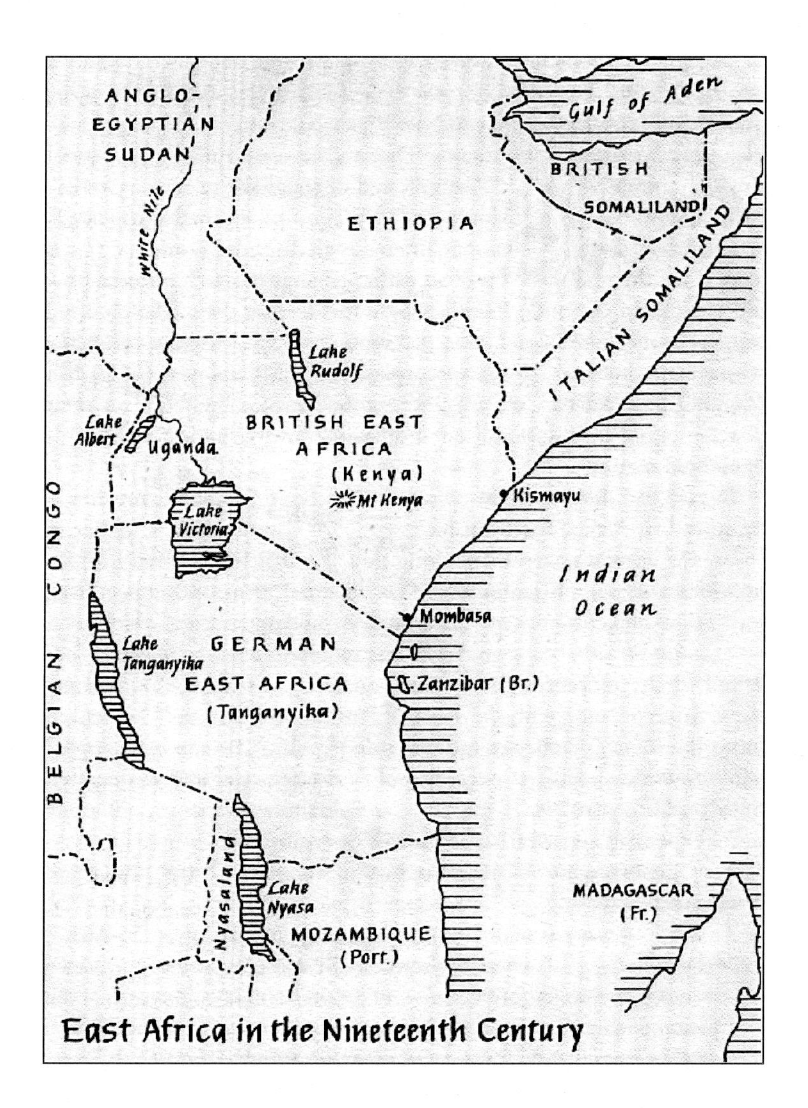

Lord Delamere's party trekked for a thousand miles from British Somaliland to British East Africa.

after two years Hugh returned to Vale Royal, his mother at first failing to recognise the emaciated, red-bearded figure limping from the train at the local railway station. There was much to discuss, not least the Vale Royal estate on the verge of bankruptcy, a truth that can hardly have come as a surprise to Hugh, although he still railed at the trustees: "I fail to see why you should tell my mother that I shall be broke in three years. It only bothers her and, as she is never here now, how could she have any influence over me?"

For a while, and without getting the better of his restlessness, he did manage to settle at Vale Royal and, tame though it must have been after his African adventures, he vigorously pursued his English passion for fox-hunting. In spite of having served with the Cheshire Yeomanry Cavalry he was never a good horseman and on one fraught hunting day he actually took thirteen falls, the last into the canal at Waverton. Later in the season his luck ran out altogether and, carried from the field on a gate, he lay on his back for six

The Cheshire Yeomanry Cavalry regularly camped on Hugh Delamere's Plovers Moss land at Oakmere.

months at Vale Royal suffering serious spinal injuries. On another occasion two gamekeepers saved him from drowning when he fell from his boat whilst duck shooting on the estate's Petty Pool, but that was Hugh Delamere, courageous, foolhardy and often too crazy for his own good.

At this time he liked to drive a four-in-hand carriage and over some triviality or other once threw down the reins and allowed the horses to bolt out of control through the village of Whitegate. Only the quick intervention of his passenger prevented a fatal accident. Nor did he endear himself to a would-be member of staff making his way from Winsford to Vale Royal for a job interview just as his lordship happened to ride past at breakneck speed and, without glance or apology, showered him with mud. In those days the rich in their castles did not generally give an inch to lesser mortals at their gates, but this man was having none of it and defiantly turned on his heels, declaring he was not going to work for that arrogant young bugger. However this was an exception. Throughout his life the communities around Vale Royal generally viewed Hugh Lord Delamere with great affection.

Romantic myth has it, that whilst convalescing from his riding accident, he met and fell in love with a nobleman's daughter, Florence Cole, who nursed him back to health whilst staying as a guest at Vale Royal. All rather convenient it probably didn't happen quite like that. A slender beauty, carefree and high-spirited, Florence was a lover of art, music, dancing and society, pleasures alien to Hugh, an extraordinarily plain and socially unfriendly Peer of the Realm, who effectively found himself a wife without, in the conventional sense, having to make much of an effort. In any case they were probably already acquainted as Florence, with her sisters and brothers, including Berkeley and Galbraith Cole, often stayed on the Vale Royal estate with their father, Lowry Egerton Cole, the 4th Earl of

The Earl of Enniskillen, Florence's father.

Enniskillen, who was a major figure in Cheshire hunting circles and most seasons would take up residence in one of Lord Delamere's prestigious properties, Pettypool House, Cassia Lodge or Heyesmere, the latter a former dower house converted into a hunting lodge.

Since before he acceded to the earldom, Lowry Egerton Cole had been a close friend of the Prince of Wales (Edward VII) and in their younger days they became jointly implicated in a paternity scandal involving a child born to the wife of Sir Charles Mordaunt, a Member of Parliament. Mordaunt sued for divorce on the grounds of his wife's confession of having had affairs with both the Prince and Lowry Egerton Cole, an allegation that rocked Victorian society. In the end, to avoid the Prince's appearance in court, Cole took the proverbial rap and admitted to fathering the child. Mordaunt got his divorce and, coincidentally, went on to wed Hugh Delamere's cousin. His first wife, Harriet, spent the rest of her life in private lunatic asylums, whilst the love child ended up as the Marchioness of Bath.

The unsavoury Mordaunt case occurred nine years before Florence's birth and only one or two salaciously inclined newspapers bothered to mention it when she walked up the aisle with Hugh Delamere at St Paul's Church, Knightsbridge. An aristocratic jamboree for the great and the good it was one of society's weddings of

Cassia Lodge, Whitegate where Edward Prince of Wales stayed as a guest of the Earl of Enniskillen.

Pettypool House, Sandiway, another Vale Royal estate residence used by the Earl of Enniskillen. Demolished after the Second World War.

the year and afterwards over five-hundred gifts were displayed at a reception at the Cadogan Square home of Florence's uncle. A week later Hugh and Florence, the fourth Lady Delamere, were welcomed home to Vale Royal by the bells of Whitegate Church and the cheers of estate workers and villagers who thronged the Hartford driveway which was bedecked with flags, bunting and triumphal arches.

Lady Florence Cole became the 4th Lady Delamere.

Three days of festivities followed, including a splendid luncheon and presentation of gifts from the estate tenantry and local dignitaries representing the towns of Northwich and Winsford. There was much to celebrate and those who had feared for the future were reassured. Nothing was going to disturb the tranquillity and rhythm of Vale Royal and the centuries-old story of the Cholmondeleys.

5

The Reckless Adventurer

"HE who has tasted honey will return to the honey-pot." So goes a Swahili proverb and when Hugh, Lord Delamere, married in July 1899, he was already planning a further trip to East Africa. One more look, perhaps under the guise of an overseas' honeymoon, collect specimens for the British Museum and then he would settle down to his responsibilities at Vale Royal. Well, that's what he promised Lady Florence.

Hugh Delamere could not resist the pull of Africa.

Since his last visit, Britain was making rapid progress constructing the hugely expensive Ugandan Railway, just short of six-hundred miles to link the Indian Ocean with Lake Victoria, and when the newly-weds arrived at the port of Mombasa, the line had reached a bleak and overcrowded transit camp called Nairobi, or Tinville, a haphazard settlement of huts and shanties in an hitherto desolate area of swampland. The word "Nairobi" means, in Masai, "cold" and even with the arrival of the railway it remained a windswept watering hole for thousands of wild animals.

The Delameres, accompanied by a taxidermist and sixty Swahili porters, set off from Mombasa on a three-day rail journey that would take them through untamed and threatening country, so dangerous the train could not run after dark and two nights had to be spent in sidings in the middle of nowhere. Florence must have wondered what she had let herself in for when told construction of the railway had almost been abandoned due to twenty-eight Indian navvies having fallen prey to man-eating lions. Then there were the tsetse flies to contend with and tribesmen who knew nothing of the outside world and wanted to make war as they believed their power would end when a great iron snake devoured their land.

Unscathed, Lord and Lady Delamere eventually reached their destination twenty-five miles short of Nairobi, but what was to follow was certainly no picnic as they set out to explore the interior. Both suffered bouts of malaria and at one stage the entire party had to hunker down for over a month in an isolated camp when two Swahili porters contracted suspected smallpox. Florence later wrote in her diary: "It was not a very pleasant place. It was about the most arid spot on the whole plain. Dust devils whirled round our camp, and ticks abounded. And to be within a measurable distance of an Indian coolie is very disagreeable."

Afterwards, except for a brief interlude to welcome in the 20th century on the shore of Lake Naivasha, the slog continued unabated as Delamere, little thought for his wife, demanded ever longer, tedious marches across the famine-stricken Rift Valley in the midst of which, shortly before her twenty-second birthday, Florence announced she was pregnant and by the summer they were back in England to celebrate the birth of a son and heir, Thomas Pitt Hamilton Cholmondeley.

Once again Delamere tried to make a fist of living the life of a country squire but East Africa had well and truly seduced him and all he could stand at Vale Royal was two years. During this otherwise relatively uneventful period he became entangled in a bitter feud with his local council when he announced he was closing an ancient road across the Vale Royal estate, what most everybody else thought was a public right of way between the Round Lodge at Sandiway and Monkey Lodge at Whitegate.

Community protests erupted and scores of witnesses lined up in opposition, but it was to no avail. Expensive counsel ensured Delamere's victory at Chester Assizes and for a while there was considerable local resentment.[1] Altogether odd and unnecessary, the case highlighted Delamere's uncompromising attitude, a trait that remained with him throughout his life. Bred into the upper class he was the last person on earth to shy from a matter of principle, or a fight with a gaggle of cap-doffing cottagers, farm labourers and shopkeeper councillors, and it was hardly surprising he would later take on the mantle of settlers' leader in East Africa. Delamere was just the man to deal with autocratic officials. Yet at Vale Royal he did not wear the cloak of Lord of the Manor any more readily than the straight-jacket of Victorian England thrust upon him when his father died in 1887.

Fired by a bold, driving energy and an insatiable thirst for excitement, he needed to push himself to the limit of his capability, and farming and estate management in leafy Cheshire was decidedly unattractive and unfulfilling. On top of that his finances were in a parlous state and England was reeling from the fag end of agricultural depression brought on by poor harvests and emerging American imports. Having seen the future in East Africa's great latent wealth he was prepared to relinquish all his ties in England to further its development. And so, shortly before Christmas 1902, leaving their son in the care of a nanny, Lord and Lady Delamere set off to seek a new life. To mark their departure, the largest shoot ever

1. Lord Delamere formally stopped the road and then immediately allowed the public to use it as a permissive footpath, i.e. closed on a set day each year to maintain its private status. The annual one-day closure was never properly implemented and over fifty years of unhindered common usage the well-used footpath became a public right of way. It was closed altogether by Sandiway Golf Club, the present owners of the former New Park.

Circa 1908: The controversial road at the Round Lodge entrance. The boy is thought to be Lord and Lady Delamere's son Thomas.

staged on the Vale Royal estate was organised, the local newspaper reporting the guns of the gentry had brought home a "capital bag" of 1,213 pheasants, wild duck and rabbits.

Delamere was dreaming of a settlement in the East African highlands, a miniature new dominion a little like New Zealand, and he was determined to play a part in opening up the country. At first he toyed with the idea of joining the British Crown service and he was actually offered a role by the governor. However, too much of a rebel to immerse himself in bureaucratic inertia, he declined. Instead he turned to farming and a life that would test his endurance and every sinew of his being. Land grants from the Crown were available beyond imagination and with his taste for reckless adventure Delamere's CV fitted to a tee, even if he was ridiculously short of liquid capital. However his first two applications to the governor were rejected, one deemed too far from a population centre, the other likely to ignite conflict with Masai tribesmen. Finally he was allocated a 99-year lease on 100,000 acres of virgin bush and forest at Njoro in the Great Rift Valley, and this he named Equator Ranch as the line of the Equator ran through one corner. Most government officials in East Africa thought him a fool to saddle himself with useless land and, in the fulness of time, they were proved correct.

Livingstone's meeting with Stanley had occurred less than thirty years before and large regions of the African continent were still unknown to Europeans, and in Delamere's eyes East Africa was wholly primitive. Its scattered peoples, frequently nomadic and separated into hostile tribes, were ignorant of the outside world and of such simple devices as the plough and the wheel, but he was not put off and agreed to pay the Crown £200 annual rent plus £5,000 on improving the land during his first five years of occupation. In fact, he ended up spending eight times more than he was officially required.

It was a huge financial commitment and the Vale Royal estate soon began to pay the price as he demanded livestock, implements and even farm workers to be shipped to Equator Ranch. First to arrive was a present from the estate, a prize Shorthorn bull, Vale Victor II, which before it succumbed to pneumonia, fathered eighty calves, the nucleus of many of modern Kenya's grade herds. Delamere's demands, a trickle initially, soon became a torrent, everything dispatched through his agent's office in Whitegate village, what was aptly christened Njoro Cottage. His agent, Major Joseph Pybus Jackson, must have dreaded opening his mail:

> I want you to get me the following – 6 Ryeland rams, 1 Ryeland ram (best class), 10 Ryeland ewes, 2 Lincoln rams, 2 Border Leicester rams, 2 Romney Marsh rams. I want them as good as possible for the money, in both meat and wool...
> Send 2 good Yorkshire boars of the large bacon-producing sort from a good herd, and four sows of

> the same breed. Also 3 turkey cocks, 12 turkey hens, 2 Aylesbury drakes, 10 Aylesbury ducks, 2 good ganders, 10 good geese, 2 cock pheasants, 6 hen pheasants. The pheasants must be very tame when sent...
>
> I want you to engage a shepherd. He must not be an uneducated bumpkin as things differ greatly in a new country and new things have to be learned. A man cannot learn sheep unless he has been accustomed to them all his life...
>
> I want you to get me 1 Shorthorn bull, 2 Shorthorn cows, 1 Hereford bull, 2 Hereford cows. Please understand that I want first-class stuff, healthy, and as good as can be got for the money.

And on it went with Delamere utterly committed to taming Equator Ranch. He seldom mentioned where payment was to come from, or the cost and logistics of shipping livestock halfway round the world. These were mere trifles in the greater scheme as disease began to annihilate swathes of his 15,000 sheep and cattle, whilst most of his crops failed miserably on land that had never previously been cultivated and was seriously deficient in minerals. Beset by a complex set of problems, the causes and cures unknown, he experimented relentlessly to find the answers and by 1908 he'd established a dairy at Equator Ranch, one small harbour of refuge in an otherwise ocean of failure and frustration, and fresh butter was dispatched daily to Mombasa. About this time a London-based magazine published an evocative account describing the Ugandan Railway and, briefly, Delamere's exploits at Njoro:

> At Mombasa the heat is tropical but for 364 miles the railway climbs uphill until at Escapement the track is 7,390ft above sea level. Then it descends. On reaching Nairobi which is 5,550ft above sea level you find yourself in a delightful climate resembling that of Southern Europe. The lowest temperature recorded is about 49 degrees Fahrenheit. Here you begin to appreciate what the East African Highlands are. Nairobi, the capital of East African Protectorate, is a busy, go-ahead place, though, from an architectural point of view, distinctly ugly, but the country round it is beautiful. From Nairobi the railway travels up a steep gradient through rich forests and beyond you find you have reached the highest point and are going downhill again. After travelling nearly a hundred miles down the slope you come to Njoro. Here the scenery is in parts very English. No wonder East Africa is growing in favour with Englishmen who have some capital to spend in buying and developing land in this corner of the Empire. Here at Njoro is Lord Delamere's estate. Lord Delamere is described as the one man in British East Africa to whom a great many settlers look for advice and help. At the farmstead, which is about a quarter of an hour's drive from Njoro Station, extensive cultivation has been carried on. The record of his struggle in the face of heavy odds can hardly be matched in the history of pioneer farmers.

In fact, Delamere was on the brink of financial ruin but he refused to be broken and, when he looked back on his years at Equator Ranch, he admitted: "I managed to get rid of £40,000 and had for a time to live on about £200 a year until a return began to materialise."

To sustain his farm, indeed his very existence, he was forced to raise additional funds from banks, life insurance policies and, most notably, by further mortgaging the Vale Royal estate and hocking off most of the contents of a magnificent library of rare books and manuscripts collected principally by his grandfather, the 1st Baron. Indeed at one stage, and clearly desperate, he accepted £1,000 from a man in Nairobi on the security of six-hundred sheep. Yet somehow he managed to acquire a second ranch, Soysambu, 48,000 acres on the western shore of Lake Elmenteita, twelve miles from Nakuru railway station and seventy miles from Nairobi. The land was better than at Equator Ranch, but not that much better. It was waterless and dry, "The Place of the Rock" to the Masai, and more tough times lay ahead.

Njoro Cottage, Lord Delamere's Whitegate estate office. The name arose from the branding of "Njoro" on the packing cases. Now known as October Lodge.

6
Guiding Star

DAIRY farming, sheep and pig farming, cross-breeding, crops, timber, even ostrich feathers for the fashion industry, Delamere the risk-taker, the innovator, never lost faith as he tried everything to make his new ranch pay, although all still had to be found by trial and error and dogged effort as there was no precedent to follow. Wheat growing was one of his major ventures, using a thousand bullocks to plough furrows three miles long, was an exhausting task for man and beast and it was one he personally undertook as he pushed himself to the extremes, unsparingly to tame the land. Binders and threshers were imported at great expense, only for the crop to be infected leaving him further up to his ears in debt. Lesser men

Cattle ranching at Soysambu in 1908.

would have called it a day, but not Delamere and, setting up his own laboratory, he discovered a new strain of wheat that led to him to establish a profitable flour-mill. He was also chiefly responsible for installing the country's first pipeline and cold store. Profit may have been his personal motivation, but underneath it all his ideal, his guiding star, was the country's development and on this he always set his course.

One of his workers at Soysambu said of him: "It was a hard life but an enjoyable one. Delamere was exacting to a degree, hardly ever satisfied and gave one the most terrific jabs in the most tender spots. On the other hand if one was in the right he would always climb down and apologise. He had the kindest of hearts provided one was prepared to devote the whole of one's energy to his interest, there was nothing he would not do for one. Despite his roaring temper I was devoted to him and so were all his natives."

Nobody ever really fathomed Delamere who, irascible and confrontational as ever, was by now the accepted leader of the settlers and able to exert great influence in politics and society, though he still refused to shirk from a fight as government officials discovered when he threatened to burn down a land office after they short-changed him over the building of his flour-mill. Not without justification, it was said even the police kept away from Delamere's land.

When he had first started farming at Equator Ranch there were fewer than a hundred European settlers but within a few years numbers began to multiply, principally due to his personal offer of free plots of 640 acres (one square mile) to better-off Brits, those who at least had sufficient wherewithal to take a gamble. The land, he insisted, was rich, easily cleared and cultivated, capable of producing three or four crops per year, and there were good markets via the Ugandan Railway. "I am going to prove to you all this is White Man's Country," he pledged.

Waxing lyrical he wrote: "Beautiful, I say, is the country. There are enormous timber trees, evergreen grasses, and clovers perennial. Streams abound, and the climate is temperate. It will grow anything, yes, anything, and to my mind it is a chance in a thousand for a man with a little money. Settlers in the country say that it compares with the very best of New Zealand. There is a good living for a man with £100 or £200 to start himself with. Coffee, potatoes, British vegetables, wheat, oats, barley, roots, British fruits etc all grow splendidly without irrigation. Any man who brings a letter from my agent will get a good allotment. I will see to it myself. Other land can be bought at threepence per acre per annum for fifteen years at which time it becomes the settler's own property. My opinion is that there are fortunes for any of the early settlers who are worth anything."

Delamere next began browbeating aristocratic British acquaintances into buying large estates where they could recreate a society that mirrored their fantasy of manorial Europe and soon they began to arrive on the Ugandan Railway, the prosaically named "Lunatic Express" – the Masai called it the "Iron Snake".

Amongst the first of the new arrivals were Lady Florence's brothers, Berkeley and Galbraith Cole, who had spent holidays on the Vale Royal estate when their father, the Earl of Enniskillen, stayed for the hunting. With Delamere's assistance, Berkeley Cole founded the Muthaiga Country Club, the pink stucco "Moulin Rouge of Africa" on the outskirts of the fledgling town of Nairobi. Cole wanted a place run on the lines of an exclusive London gentleman's club where a bell would summon a drink on a spotless tray, and at the club's inaugural dinner Lord Delamere sat at the head of fourteen elite settlers. With its own golf course, squash courts, croquet lawn and ballroom, the Muthaiga evolved into the favoured haunt of the small clique of Happy Valleyers, infamous for champagne, sundowners, drugs and wife swapping.

A dandy of dry wit, Berkeley Cole was a close friend of Denys Finch Hatton and his partner Karen Blixen, author of *Out of Africa*. Blixen famously recalled that whilst staying as their houseguest Cole would drink a bottle of champagne every morning at eleven and complain if the glasses were not of the finest quality. When he died at the age of forty-three she lamented: "An epoch in the history of the colony came to an end with him. The yeast was out of the bread of the land."

Berkeley Cole, founder of the infamous Muthaiga Club. He was Lady Florence's brother.

Berkeley Cole's brother, Galbraith , a former officer in the 10th Hussars, was a different kettle of fish and far more controversial. He moved to the colony in 1905 and took up farming 30,000 acres Delamere gave to him adjoining Soysambu Ranch. Here, in 1911, Cole shot and killed an African labourer he said was sheep stealing and, though as guilty as hell, a jury took just five minutes to acquit him. Cole escaped the noose but, to the fury of Lord Delamere, the court ordered his deportation. Delamere was visiting Cheshire at the time and fired off letters to English newspapers protesting that as Cole had been found not guilty, deportation was unfair and unjust. Nevertheless, Cole was deported and it took the intervention of his mother, the Countess of Enniskillen, and his sister, Lady Florence Delamere, to persuade the government to allow him to return. Years later Galbraith Cole married a niece of the former British Prime Minister Lord Balfour. In 1929, wheelchair-bound and blind in one eye, he shot himself.

Galbraith Cole's murder trial was a sham. A jury of white men was never going to convict a white man and that's the way it was with Delamere and the settlers who embodied the prevailing belief in the British Empire's omnipotence to expand and last for ever, that it would be strong and permanent in the highlands of East Africa. An historical fact, the future yet to be written, this was a view shared by young Winston Churchill, Parliamentary Under-Secretary for the Colonies, who stayed at Soysambu and asserted that the highlands should be the exclusive preserve of white settlers. Delamere got on famously with Churchill and in red jackets and white breeches they went English hunting behind English foxhounds in pursuit of African jackal.

A long way from Vale Royal: The Muthaiga Club founded by Berkeley Cole. Its first president was Lord Delamere.

7

Two huts and Africa

THE most tragic figure in Lord Delamere's wild adventure was, undoubtedly, Lady Florence. Named after her father's family seat, Florence Court, in County Fermanagh, she had grown up to a life of entitlement and ease and no matter how much she had prepared herself she could never have envisaged the harshness of their first home at Equator Ranch, a remote, native-style grass hut in the middle of Africa. Delamere, barely able to walk following yet another riding accident, had to be carried there on a stretcher and thousands of miles from Vale Royal, without doctor or domestic servants, Florence, the fourth Lady Delamere, was left to devotedly nurse him in the most primitive of conditions.

Her eventual "reward" was a windowless wooden shack with a beaten earth floor and not even a proper door. She did her best by introducing a few incongruous pieces of fine furniture from Vale Royal, mahogany sideboards and valuable oak tallboys, to stand at drunken angles on uneven floors. Her husband showed little interest in the mix of ramshackle and grandeur and how she must have reflected on the life of luxury she had cast aside to become the first Lady Delamere of the 20th century. In her monumental two-volume work *White Man's Country*, author Elspeth Huxley paints a vivid picture of what Florence had to endure at Equator Ranch: "Delamere's huts were planted down in the open with no more disturbance to the natural panorama than the shaving of a little patch of grass. As far as the eye could see there was no sign of human life. There was nothing to soften the immensity or to give a sense of proportion to the landscape. Just two huts, and Africa."

Having recovered from his latest health setback, farming was an immense, financial sapping challenge for Delamere who, every day, would leave his bed before sunrise to breakfast by the light of a hurricane lamp whilst his favourite tune "All Aboard for Margate" rattled out on his wind-up gramophone. Then it would be on to the ploughing with his Masai workers; he was close to the Masai, learned their language and embraced their culture, but as *White Mischief* author James Fox notes, he could never have been accused of going native as he was far too grand for that. Enormous hat, hair flowing around his shoulders to protect him against the sun, he would be on the go from dawn to dusk.

At one point, and having reached the end of his resources, he was forced to return to England to raise money to carry on and whilst he was away poor Florence plunged into the maelstrom of farm management which she undertook with her customary enthusiasm. Letters she sent to Delamere highlight what she had to put up with: "I wish you had told me to look after the pigs… I have been ploughing with the bullocks but not to my satisfaction… The rain has been awful and the cold intense. I hope you won't be annoyed but I couldn't stand it any longer and have bought a little house and have hired a carpenter to build it. I could not stand the cold any longer."

Their marriage marginally improved when they moved to Soysambu and a proper home, but it remained far from easy and Florence would often become the butt of her husband's vicious tongue and foul temper that would kick into overdrive at the latest farming setback, or chronic money problem, when he would peevishly insist on scrutinizing every item of her household and personal expenditure. Florence's brother Galbraith Cole found the entire set-up depressing: "I can't help thinking my sister must have hated it," he said. "There's somehow a barrenness about Delamere's surroundings that I can't explain."

Florence Lady Delamere.

Elephant, leopard and lion roamed the vast land and European settlement was sparse but Delamere didn't seem to give his wife a second thought and, sometimes for weeks on end, he would simply leave her to get on with it as he pursued his larger than life existence as unofficial head of the settlers, inaugural member of the settlers' own Parliament, the Legislative Council, President of the Colonists' Association, President of the Farmers' Association, President of the Muthaiga Club, President of the East African Turf Club, organiser of

Old Etonian reunions. He rarely stopped except for his one great pleasure, Nairobi Race Week, a twice-yearly gathering for business as much as sport. For many of the settlers – but not Delamere – slow horses and fast women were obligatory.

During his many absences, whether from Equator Ranch or Soysambu, poor Florence had to take over running the farm and a lonely, monotonous task it was, a constant grind of hard, exhausting work and, sometimes, she would fear for her safety such as when local tribes became restless and she had to arm herself with a shot-gun and cartridges. Looking back on his ancestor's life, Andrew the 7th Earl of Enniskillen wrote: "She (Florence) was unable to stand up to the rigours and harshness of pioneering in Kenya and it helped none that she was left alone for long periods of time in an almost

In his enormous sunhat Lord Delamere heads the Colonists' Association.

uninhabited tract of land with no close neighbours while her husband was building the nation."

Her own health failing, Florence bore it all with fortitude and her cheerfulness and courage was admired by all those who came into contact with her, including Theodore Roosevelt who stayed for a fortnight at Soysambu during a Safari to mark the ending of his term of office as 26th President of the United States. Afterwards he wrote to her: "I know that you and D have the large outlook, that your own success comes second to the feeling that you have taken the lead in adding to the Empire the last province than can be added to the white man's part of it. He has rendered to East Africa and therefore Great Britain a literally incalculable service. I only wish that in England itself there was a fuller appreciation of the service."

Whenever there was an opportunity to visit her son in England, Florence would set off on an exhausting sea passage via the east coast of Africa, the Red Sea, the Gulf of Aden, the Suez Canal and, eventually, home via Marseille or Gibraltar. In 1908 Lord Delamere accompanied her, although parental duty was far from uppermost in his mind. Heavily in debt to the banks, his ever-dependable milch cow, the Vale Royal estate, was running dry and his great hope lay in selling part, or all, of it, a proposition his mother, the redoubtable Dowager Lady Augusta, vehemently opposed. His response was to flee back to Soysambu leaving Florence to stand in for him at the formal opening of Whitegate village hall that had been built on a small plot of land he'd given to the community. Apologising to the gathering and clearly embarrassed, Florence understatedly remarked that her husband had been forced to return to East Africa in order to attend to "serious business matters".

Before leaving England Delamere gave an interview to the *Manchester Courier* and further extolled the virtues of East Africa. Sheep and pig rearing were likely to prove profitable, he said, and everything grew marvellously in the highlands. Two thousand ostriches provided feathers for the fashion trade, wattle bark for the tanning industry, and a good class of American cotton could be grown. His only words of caution were to advise against anyone of "small means" trying to settle in the country.

Three years later, his mother, the Dowager Lady Augusta, was dead and suddenly, without warning, tenancy termination notices dropped on seventy Vale Royal estate farmers, cottagers and small traders, many from generations of families who had lived for centuries under the paternal wing of the Cholmondeleys. One thousand acres, farms, smallholdings, dwellings and shops were to go under the hammer on the pretext of ensuring a bright future for the remaining estate. Major Jackson, Delamere's agent, wrote to the condemned tenants:

"I have to enclose herewith Lord Delamere's intention to terminate your tenancy. In doing so I am desired to explain that his Lordship has decided to sell the outlying portion of his estate which lies on the Over and Winsford side of the Cheshire Lines Railway. His Lordship is extremely reluctant to part with any portion of his estate, or to disturb his tenants, but for the purposes of development of other portions of the Vale Royal estate he finds that it has now become necessary to dispose of part of the property."

Delamere was not interested in developing the remaining estate – it could go to the devil, he said. His creditors were closing in and he needed every spare penny he could lay his hands on, even the valuable 17th century mace his father had permanently loaned to Over Council for ceremonial purposes. Demanding its return, his intention was clear when he took it with him to East Africa. Fortunately he didn't manage to sell, or he changed his mind and in 1946 his son handed it back to the town.

The Vale Royal estate sale of 1912, shortly before Christmas at

Lord Delamere's sister Sybil.

the Royal Hotel, Crewe, realized £56,000, equivalent to £4 million at current values. Many tenants, unable to afford to purchase their properties, were left deeply disenchanted, although Delamere's African adventure affected none more than his own sister, Sybil. Five years married to Horse Guards' officer, Algernon Burnaby, she was a divorcee with a teenage son and she relied heavily on a stipend from a £10,000 Vale Royal trust set up by her father, the 2nd Baron. However, under her brother's care the income had diminished to practically nothing and she was in dire financial straits, struggling to maintain the house her mother had provided for her in Belgravia. A friend took up Sybil's plight and appealed directly to Delamere, but it did no good – he was focused, he said, on his own life, his own ambitions and desires in East Africa. Soon afterwards, Sybil fell from a third-floor window at her home and it was never firmly established whether it had been a terrible accident, or suicide. A Scotland Yard report stated that housemaids had tried to hold her back, but she had cried "Don't, let me go".

In 1911, the year of Sybil's tragic death, Florence returned to Cheshire for two years prior to young Thomas taking up his place at Eton. Mother and son settled on the Vale Royal estate at Heyesmere, the hunting lodge where she had spent her own childhood holidays. Universally popular, gracious and generous, Lady Florence went out of her way to brighten the lives of everyone around her, making gifts to the poor, sharing in the joys and sorrows of estate tenants and immersing herself in the affairs of Mid Cheshire. All the while her health continued to deteriorate and, before long, she collapsed with a nervous breakdown. Eventually part recovered, she returned to Soysambu only to find Delamere seriously ill and, running the farm from his bed, had been ordered by doctors to convalesce in England. It was the beginning of 1914 and he had planned to attend Tarporley Hunt Club's 150th anniversary dinner hosted at Oulton Park by his neighbour Sir Philip Grey Egerton. The Marquess of Crewe, club president, and the lady patroness, Sir Henry John Delves Broughton's sister, Rosamund, of Doddington Hall, welcomed over four hundred guests to what was considered one of the most brilliant social functions ever held in Cheshire. Everybody who was anybody was there, but Lord Delamere, who had indicated he would attend, was conspicuous by his absence.

Back at Soysambu Florence was left as usual to manage the farm but, barely able to walk, it was a painful struggle and before

Vale Royal could go to the devil, said Lord Delamere.

long her heart gave out. As she lay gravely ill in a Nairobi hospital, Delamere struggled back from England and reached her bedside just two days before she died at the age of just thirty-six. It was a tragedy. Florence would have been in her prime had it not been for the rigours and hardship endured in selfless pursuit of her husband's fanatical dream. Her devotion had rarely been reciprocated.

She was buried in East Africa, although nowhere was her passing felt more acutely than in Cheshire, King George V sending a message of condolence to a memorial service held at Whitegate. Twelve months later a brass tablet was unveiled in the little church to mark the addition of a stained-glass window and tower clock dedicated to her memory. The tablet reads: "Florence Lady Delamere: This window and clock on the church tower were erected by her friends and the tenants on the Vale Royal Estate".

St Mary's Church, Whitegate, with the clock in memory of Florence Lady Delamere. On the site of a chapel connected with Vale Royal Abbey, the church dates from 1728. It was largely rebuilt by the 2nd Baron Delamere in 1874/75.

8
Winds of Change

WHEN Florence died in May 1914, A.E. Housman's steady drummer of war could be heard in the distance and there was little time for Lord Delamere to adjust. East Africa's Anglo-German border ran through two-hundred miles of unguarded frontier and he was devastated when news came through as he was dispatching cattle from Elmenteita railway station. His reaction was to walk up and down the platform swearing violently, and no wonder. The country and his own farming enterprises were at last beginning to turn the corner and war, whatever it meant, would slam everything into reverse.

Even though he was an unapologetic pacifist he immediately volunteered to take on the onerous task of leading Masai patrols to monitor enemy movements. It was a tough assignment and for six months, twelve hours a day, he was in the saddle, never sparing himself in spite of his poor health. "They were the hardest six months' work of my life," he afterwards wrote.

In the end he succumbed and, half-dead from a strained heart and malaria, he was carried back to Soysambu on an ox-cart. Later in England doctors told him that he must not, in future, live in East Africa for more than three months at a stretch on account of the altitude. He ignored them and, though still physically weak at the end of the war, he vociferously immersed himself into campaigning for his adopted country to be granted Crown Colony status by the British government. As the author Elspeth Huxley commented, "There was hardly an industry in which he had not experimented, a society to which he did not belong, a political issue to which he had not joined. He loved Kenya more than he cared for his own interests, or his health, or ultimately even his life."

Someone else said of him: "His ascendancy over the settlers has been enjoyed long enough for him to expect all men – and women – to do his bidding. He is their Moses, their guide."

The winds of change were certainly sweeping over Africa and Kenya Colony was officially born in 1920, a new age and new hopes, but it came at terrible personal cost to Delamere who was near stone-broke after struggling through seven gruelling years of health issues, his wife's death, the economic stagnation of the war, and the endless political and bureaucratic issues associated with cleaving self-government from Britain. As ever, he was forced to turn to Vale Royal to bail him out, this time borrowing against what was left of the family trust, and this just about saved him from going under until a chink of light slowly began to appear for his evolving farming enterprises in Kenya. It meant, by the mid-1920s, his annual profits were topping £30,000, almost all of it destined to pay crippling and continuous mortgages and overdrafts.

Many are the tales told of Delamere's eccentricity and his sharp tongue. In his earlier days railway officials frequently roused his ire, none more than the local stationmaster who dispatched an urgent telegraph to Nairobi: "The Lord has kicked me. Please advise." On another occasion Delamere, accompanied by a bull terrier bitch and her four puppies, boarded a train without paying. The stationmaster wired to Nairobi: "The Lord is on the train with one bitch and four sons of bitches. No tickets. Please collect."

Depending who happens to be looking through the viewfinder, there are accounts of him shooting out the streetlights on a Nairobi thoroughfare, riding his horse into the Norfolk Hotel and turning the tables into a steeplechase course, issuing his Masai herdsmen with umbrellas as protection from the sun and lashing rain. Later, in his twilight years, he would rather absurdly play golf at the head of a small procession of retainers, one carrying his clubs, the second his field glasses and a dozen balls, the third a large box of cigars. How Delamere would have enjoyed the irony of Vale Royal's transformation into a 21st century golf club.

Lord Delamere in the late 1920s.

One thing is for sure, he never lost his puerile sense of humour, nor his eccentricity. Growing older he began to mellow and beyond politics he was certainly less confrontational. Even so, his vitality continued as farmer, politician and leader of local society. He didn't seem to require sleep and would sometimes dance all night, breakfast at sunrise and drive home to issue the day's orders for work on the ranch. He would then be back in Nairobi by ten o'clock for meetings that would last all day.

What did begin to hit him hard was fourteen years of widowhood and though he tended to avoid most of the revelries associated with the in-crowd, he turned his thoughts to marriage. The new woman in his life, Lady Gwladys Markham, was an energetic divorced mother of three, twenty-seven years his junior and financially expectant. Pale skinned with jet-black hair she was thirty-one, glamorous and in her prime, whilst Delamere, his health rapidly careering downhill, had gone well past his sell-by date. Mismatch it may have been and yet the arrangement suited both parties – Delamere had found himself an attractive younger woman to share his life, whilst Gwladys had landed a husband of enormous status and apparent wealth.

How Delamere and Gwladys Markham came to meet is unclear, but there was certainly a hunting connection from way back. Her maternal great-grandfather was the 3rd Marquess of Anglesey and one of his sons was Gwladys's maternal grandfather, Lord Berkeley Paget, of Blakemere Hall, Sandiway. From here, around the turn of the 20th century, Lord Berkeley and his elder brother, Lord Alexander (Dandy) Paget, of Bunbury, would frequently ride to hounds with Delamere and also attend Tarporley Hunt Club dinners together. Dandy Paget's son, that is to say Gwladys's second cousin, went on to become the 6th Marquess of Anglesey of Plas Newyyd.

Gwladys (her Christian name spelt with a "w" and therefore posher than common Gladys) was the eldest daughter of wealthy newspaper and banking magnate Rupert Beckett and, from toddler age, photographs of her regularly appeared in society magazines like *Tatler*. By her late teens she was, naturally, socialising in the highest circles and the *Sunday Pictorial* said of her in 1915: "It has become the fashion to voice regrets for the war debutante in these times. But nobody need feel sorry for Miss Gwladys Beckett who is nearly eighteen and is a debutante of the near future. She is a most charming girl and possesses a charming mother, tall and very distinguished in style."

In 1920, at a top-drawer London wedding attended by a guest list running into hundreds, including the British Prime Minister David Lloyd George, Gwladys had married Sir Charles Markham of Newstead Abbey, Nottinghamshire, a "waster" according to her friends. And so it proved when they moved to Kenya and Gwladys gave birth to a son. Two further children followed but the

Gwladys's grandfather Lord Berkeley Paget (2nd left) with his brothers Lord Alexander Paget and Henry Paget, the 4th Marquess of Anglesey. The younger man was to become the 5th Marquess.

Markhams were both conspicuously unfaithful and in 1927 they were granted a divorce, euphemistically on the grounds of Sir Charles' "misconduct" – a Charing Cross Hotel waiter testifying to his "indiscretions".

Sir Charles went on to wed an exotic dancer, whilst his younger brother, Mansfield Markham, married Kenyan-based Beryl Clutterbuck, an impetuous and single-minded young woman whose father had once worked for Lord Delamere. Very much part of Nairobi's Happy Valley set, Beryl's lovers had included the Duke of Gloucester, an affair Buckingham Palace embarrassingly paid to hush-up. After marrying Markham, Beryl went on to make aviation history as the first woman to fly solo from England to North America.

Lady Gwladys Markham.

And so Lord Delamere's bride-to-be, Lady Gwladys Markham, was no stranger when she pitched up in Kenya for the wedding in 1928. Prior to the nuptials she stayed with the Governor, Sir Edward Grigg, who formally gave her away at the ceremony in St Andrew's Scottish Church, Nairobi. A fellow member of the Tarporley Hunt Club, Jock Delves Broughton and his wife Vera, were amongst the guests, and a neighbouring rancher, Lord Francis Scott, Delves Broughton's former Irish Guards' commanding officer, stood as best man. A reception followed at Government House prior to Delamere and Gwladys setting off for England on a honeymoon that would have far-reaching consequences, redefine the feudal landscape of Mid Cheshire and, in one way or another, affect every single resident for miles around.

The newly-weds after the ceremony in Nairobi.

9

The Prince and the Lady

IN a remorselessly changing world it was with great sorrow that Lord Delamere followed from afar the break-up and financial decline of many of Britain's aristocratic estates, their plight hastened by war, insidious death duties and the evolving stockmarket slump. One of the most tragic cases, and it touched him deeply, concerned Oulton Hall, the Cheshire seat of Sir Philip Grey Egerton. The Cholmondeley and Grey Egerton families had lived cheek by jowl for centuries at Whitegate and Little Budworth and Sir Philip's twin sons, Philip and Rowland, pageboys at Delamere's marriage to Florence Cole in 1899, had both been cut down in the Great War killing fields of France – Rowland in the first weeks of the conflict, Philip in the final days.

Without a direct heir Sir Philip had lost interest in the estate and on St Valentine's Day 1926, whilst being rented to a Manchester industrialist, majestic Oulton Hall was reduced to charred rubble in a devastating conflagration that claimed six lives, five of them members of Sir Philip's estate workforce. The sixth victim was a Tarporley fireman who left a widow and eight children. All had perished in a valiant if somewhat rash attempt to salvage priceless paintings and artefacts, and at the inquest Sir Philip's agent painted a grim scene:

"There were fifteen of us in the drawing room and the saloon, and some were mounted on ladders when someone shouted a warning. A huge crack was spotted in the ceiling and before any of us could make our escape the massive ceiling and rafters came crashing down. Flames and dense smoke enveloped us and the screams

Oulton Hall, one of the crowning glories of Cheshire.

were terrible. Fortunately most of us escaped through the French windows."

The cause of the fire, a spark from a chimney or faulty wiring in the roofspace, was not conclusively established and great bitterness was felt amongst the families of the victims who maintained their loved ones had been ordered by the agent to re-enter the burning building. The insurance company disagreed and refused to pay out a penny of compensation, insisting they had all "volunteered".

Oulton's fate seemed symbolic in the decline of Cheshire's landed estates and, almost inevitably, Vale Royal was destined to follow when, in 1928, Lord Delamere finally resolved to rid himself of the one millstone around his neck he least cared about. For years the Vale Royal estate and its sparse income had continued in the hands of receivers and, to keep himself afloat in Kenya, he launched the then largest estate sale ever seen in the county. Five thousand acres of the "finest dairy land in the county", eighty-six farms and smallholdings, seventy country cottages and three public houses, the Blue Cap, Abbey Arms and Plough beerhouse, all came under the hammer in the town of Winsford and the surrounding villages of Oakmere, Whitegate, Delamere, Sandiway, Davenham, Moulton and Marton.

The public houses together yielded £10,000 and, with several larger farms and building plots sold privately, the total proceeds amounted to just over £125,000. In addition, through Sotheby's of London, much of the family's collection of engravings and paintings, including works by Bruegel, Rubens, Lely and Gainsborough, were auctioned. The iconic family portrait of "Diamond Pitt" may have been sold earlier.

When it was all over, the bones picked from most of the skeleton, only the great rambling house, the immediate parkland and a few hundred acres of land remained on the surface. Below ground it was a different matter as Delamere had astutely retained the mineral rights and, within a couple of years, he sold these to the Salt Union for £71,030. It remains to be seen whether the transaction was actually legal as the modern day Land Registry, probably mindful of shale gas potential, insists the mineral rights have always been vested in the Crown.

Delamere was not present to witness the death throes of the former monastic estate and centuries of family history. He had already returned to Kenya, leaving Lady Gwladys to follow in early September with her three young children. Just at this time, Edward Prince of Wales, was also setting off for Kenya and Uganda to shoot big-game, and this has given rise to a rumour that he and Gwladys were lovers whilst travelling on the same ship. Quite untrue, although it does add to the mystique of Happy Valley. Edward and Gwladys were certainly "acquainted", but she had left England a week before him and then he detoured into Egypt before arriving in Kenya on board the SS Malda.

Lord Delamere (right) with the Prince of Wales.

The Prince, accompanied by his brother, the Duke of Gloucester, did stay briefly with the Delameres although, it's fair to say, they were both more interested in the charms of the Muthaiga Club where they ordered dancing throughout the night. Impetuous whenever the mood took him, the heir to the throne then resorted to hurling gramophone records out of the ballroom window. Lady Delamere shared Edward's disdain for the overbearing conventions of polite society and, when they all attended a boisterous supper, she joined in the fun, much to the indignation of Karen Blixen, the author of *Out of Africa*: "Lady Delamere behaved scandalously. She bombarded the Prince of Wales with big pieces of bread and finished up by rushing him, overturning his chair and rolling him around the floor. I do not find that kind of thing in the least amusing, and stupid to do at a club. I do not find her particularly likeable."

As it turned out Edward did not take offence and in 1930, on his second trip to Kenya, this time to hunt elephant, he again visited the Delameres and invited them to his safari camp.

Lord Delamere had adapted well to marriage after fourteen years of widowhood, mud huts of the old days long gone, and with his companion wife Gwladys at his side, he settled more readily into home comforts after a life of furious pace dealing with complex farming enterprises, the stress of politics and, most of all, his colossal debts. However his health was giving rise to serious concern and on medical grounds he was forced to resign from the Legislative Council and yet, in spite of being a desperately sick man, he never lost his enthusiasm for the Kenyan cause, so much so he remarkably headed a deputation to an Imperial Conference in London.

Here were the prime ministers of all the dominions of the British Empire and Delamere gave them a piece of his mind at suggestions that Kenya should be placed under international control. "Englishmen out there want to remain a part of the British Empire," he stormed. In recognition of his thirty years of dedication to Kenya he was created a Knight Commander of St Michael and St George, a KCMG in the British order of chivalry. It was the first civil honour ever awarded to a Kenyan settler for services within the country.

A year later, on November 13, 1931, at the age of sixty-one, Lord Delamere passed away following a series of angina attacks. If his grandson, the 5th Baron, is correct, he died of a broken heart, brought on by his endless financial problems: "He had asked the Kenyan Farmers' Association, which he founded, for credit and they turned him down."

Leader of the settlers to the end, Delamere was, fittingly, buried in a simple grave on a rocky knoll at Soysambu, overlooking the seductive landscape he had first cast his eyes on at the close of the 19th century. A special issue of Kenya's *Government Gazette* declared him the "inspiration" for the entire development of the colony, whilst Elspeth Huxley noted: "Old-timers who had known Delamere twenty-five years ago came to the funeral in torn and stained farm clothes, shorts and khaki bush shirts. There were bearded Dutchmen, officials in white uniforms and decorations, clergymen in surplices and sun helmets. Copper-skinned Masai stalked after the procession in their short hide cloaks and oily pigtails, carrying their long spears."

The aviator Beryl Markham said: "Delamere's character had as many facets as cut stone, but each facet shone with individual brightness. His generosity was legendary, but so was his wholly unjustified anger. To him nothing was more important than the agriculture and political future of British East Africa – and so he was a serious man. Yet his gaiety and occasional abandonment to the spirit of fun, which I have often witnessed, could hardly be equalled except by an ebullient schoolboy."

Modern researchers and writers tend to be less charitable and some denounce Delamere as a megalomaniac whose ambition was to become emperor, or ruling president of a White Man's Kenya. This is abject nonsense. Yes, entitlement was seared in his psyche, and, yes, he possessed a fiery, autocratic temper and could be explosive and eccentric, but power was never his driving force. In Kenya it was always a fanatical stubbornness, a passion to guide his adopted country to a prosperous 20th century future. He was too much of a loose cannon, far too pugnacious to use politics for self-serving personal motive. During his life's fleeting moment in Kenyan history, he was a man of his time, his sincerity and integrity beyond reproach. Three media outlets spanning eighty years best sum up Delamere's impact: In 1931 the England-based magazine *Truth* commented: "More than any man he made the colony. He may sometimes have been a bit of a whirlwind, but he got things done and his name will head the first chapter of Kenya's history."

Twenty years after his death a BBC documentary series, *They Found Fame*, featured "Lord Delamere, The Man who made Kenya". A stimulating wireless narrative this told the story of his roots deep in Cheshire, a man of great resourcefulness who had become a legend, but about whom his own country knew very little: "Despite every conceivable setback, the wiry spirit of this man refused to be broken. He gave his all for Kenya and sacrificed Vale Royal for the sake of colonisation." In 2016 the *Nairobi Wire*, a leading news blog, had this to say: "When colonial history is told we often hear of the atrocities and the negatives. But modern day Kenya was built on the foundation laid by individuals like Lord Delamere. His arrival and that of the British in general may have been unwelcome, but his contribution was like no other, past or present."

Lord Delamere from a portrait presented to him by settlers.

Of all the eulogies heaped on Delamere, the most discerning is also the simplest. A plaque in Whitegate Church reads: "A statesman, far seeing, daring in enterprise, undaunted by failures, he devoted his life to Kenya and her advancement." Poignantly set alongside those of his father and grandfather, he would be the last of the Cholmondeley family to be formally commemorated in the picturesque village church.

Those who claim Delamere brazenly exploited Kenya should reflect on the mind-blowing price he paid to develop and nurture what would become one of Africa's most stable economies. He invested £40,000 trying and failing to develop Equator Ranch, raised approximately £185,000 from the 1912 and 1928 Vale Royal estate sales and £70,000 from the mineral rights. Along the way he impoverished his family, peddled the treasures of his forebears and, on his death, he still owed the banks £500,000. How ever this is calculated, in today's money his total outlay amounted to the equiva-

Delamere's memorial in Whitegate Church.

lent of £25 million, all of it, directly and indirectly, steered to Kenya. What other man in history has personally invested so much in his own country, let alone one thousands of miles away?

As to Delamere's widow Lady Gwladys, and regardless of what may have been her motives for marrying a very much older man, she made him extremely happy during their short time together. She devotedly cared for him and, increasingly, he valued her advice and sound judgement. When they were briefly apart, and this resonates with his decision to sell the Vale Royal estate, he wrote to her: "I believe that you and the future of Kenya are the only things I care for."

Delamere's dream lived on through Lady Gwladys as she set out to blaze her own political trail. Many considered her an intimidating bossy bitch, others said she was egocentric, energetic, authoritarian and, for the most part, brutally frank, but then she had to be to succeed in a colonial, male-dominated arena. And succeed she did to become one of Kenya's most popular politicians. In 1934 she was elected onto the Municipal Council of Nairobi and served as a councillor until 1938 when she was chosen to be the Mayor, a post she held for three terms until 1940.

During her periods of office she was held in high esteem throughout Africa, for her anti-poverty programmes in Nairobi's ghettos, for assisting European settlers financially stranded by the Depression of the 1930s, and for turning her Nairobi residence into a wartime convalescent home which she later gave to the Red Cross Service. Awarded a CBE for services to Kenya she suffered a serious bout of typhoid, lost her looks and lapsed into moods of extreme unpredictability, once throwing a plate of bacon and eggs at another woman in the Muthaiga Club.

Lady Gwladys, the Mayor of Nairobi.

Lady Gwladys died of a stroke in February 1943. Her funeral was attended by the Governor of Kenya, her coffin carried by representatives of the country's three fighting services. Amongst the wreaths was one from General Jan Smuts, the Prime Minister of South Africa. She was buried at Soysambu near to Lord Delamere.

LORD DELAMERE'S STATUE

Following Lord Delamere's death, the Earl of Erroll promoted the idea of commemorating him by renaming Nairobi's main thoroughfare "Delamere Avenue". Later, in 1939, an eight-foot bronze statue, created by the British sculptor Kathleen Scott, Lady Kennet, was erected at the head of the street. It depicted Delamere as he was best remembered... wearing a cardigan, open shirt and flannel trousers. Plans to erect a replica statue in London were abandoned due to the outbreak of war.

10

Cheshire's Great Gatsby

Doddington Park Lodge and The Boars Head, early 20th century.

HISTORY often dwells in quiet places and, in its heyday, there were few quieter corners of Cheshire than that of Doddington Hall and its parkland close by the old London road, a few miles south east of Nantwich. Here for over five centuries lived Sir Henry John Delves Broughton's ancestors, men who had scribed their names in the chronicles of England from as early as the Battle of Poitiers when a Delves distinguished amongst the Black Prince's eight thousand who routed sixty thousand French. Later a Delves' daughter and heiress married into the Broughtons, a venerable Staffordshire family, baronets since the 17th century and directly descended from a trusted Norman knight. And so was born the Delves Broughtons, a wealthy and powerful amalgam of large estates and prestige in two counties.

In 1881 the 10th Baronet, Sir Louis Delves Broughton, married a distant cousin who died two years after giving birth to Henry John who was destined to become the 11th Baronet, the aristocrat at the centre of Kenya's infamous *White Mischief* saga. Known from a young age as "Jock", the child endured a lonely upbringing when his father remarried and he was demoted to the care of nannies and governesses at Doddington. He never get on with his stepmother and, when elevated to the hallowed corridors of Eton, his strict disciplinarian father kept him ridiculously short of money, a terrible embarrassment since it was well known his grandfather, the 9th Baronet, had recently left an estate worth over £750,000, even if most of it was secured in a family trust. At Eton young Jock, secretive and insecure, was considered a misfit, uncommunicative, overproud and, apparently, not very bright, none of which impeded his

Doddington Hall, ancestral seat of the Delves Broughtons.

progress, via Cambridge, to a military career with the Irish Guards. Tall and imposing in uniform, he was reckoned to be one of the most handsome officers in the regiment, as well as the most conceited. Seldom short of lady friends he went on to marry Vera Edyth Boscawen, the second daughter of a cash-strapped branch of a well-to-do Denbighshire family of Trevalyn Hall, Rossett, near Chester. Vera, said to be as hard as nails, lived life in the fast lane and big-game hunting was to become her passion.

For three decades Delves Broughton's father had thriftily modernised the Cheshire and Staffordshire estates and when he died he left Jock £125,000. In addition the family trust included farms, cottages, fifteen thousand acres of prime farmland, Doddington Hall, a mansion in London's Mayfair and the former Broughton family seat, Broughton Hall, an Elizabethan-style manor house near to the small market town of Eccleshall in Staffordshire. The *Chester Chronicle* said of the 10th Baronet: "His life was interwoven with the formation of an estate that is now a monument of agricultural perfection and unselfish landlordism. He is succeeded by Captain Jock who has been mainly occupied with military duties than the work of the estate, but everybody hopes and believes he will continue the wise and generous policy of his lamented father."

Wishful thinking, indeed. After years suffering his father's parsimony a wise policy was alien to "Captain Jock" who at thirty-one seemed to have it all – a prestigious title, two estates, a beautiful wife, two children and, above all, enormous land wealth. It was payback time and within weeks of laying his father to rest, in April 1914, he was selling off eight Doddington Hall farms and the entire Broughton Hall estate in Staffordshire. For good measure at this time he also, rather pretentiously, announced that like his father he was to be addressed as Sir Delves Broughton, a curious patronymic combination for someone with a British double-barrelled surname that his family had proudly used since the start of the 19th century. His correct unabbreviated title was Sir Henry John Delves Broughton.

Whatever his nomenclature preference, his plans to cash in on his inheritance were ruthless and, either by good fortune or cunning, he even managed to escape the killing fields of France. Soon after Britain declared war, and due to sail on a hot August day with his battalion of the Irish Guards, he was suddenly taken ill, apparently suffering from sunstroke, and had to be left behind to recuperate in a military hospital. All rather mysterious, it turned out to be a fortuitous escape as, within weeks, his battalion was decimated on the battlefield at Aisne. To Delves Broughton's eternal shame, Rudyard Kipling later referred to the bizarre sunstroke incident in his book, *The Irish Guards in the Great War*, one survivor recalling: "The day had not been over strenuous for a normal fit man and there can be no question of sunstroke. He was not a very bellicose gent

Broughton Hall was sold within weeks of the 10th Baronet's death.

and he was certainly never again in a service battalion." On the other hand, Delves Broughton's ever-faithful valet and batman, Charles Pegram, naturally had a different take: "Military doctors aren't idiots – they would've known if he was putting it on. He was bloody sick, that's all. Looked strong, but he wasn't."

In any event, Delves Broughton landed a cushy desk job and, though he never saw active fighting service, he was promoted to the rank of Major and then, following a car accident, discharged from the army on medical grounds.

The years immediately after the Armistice marked the start of his milk and honey days and he set off to visit Kenya colony, an almost obligatory passage for ex-army officers with a taste for adventure and nowhere to go. Top of his to-see list was, of course, Lord Delamere who pressed on him the opportunities to make a fortune on the back of the British Crown's Soldier Settlement Scheme that offered land on easy terms to former wartime servicemen. Three years later he returned and, whilst his adventurous wife was throwing herself into the excitement of big-game hunting, he purchased cattle land and a coffee plantation that, by any stretch of imagination, was a gamble as he had no intention of settling in the colony. But that was Delves Broughton in the 1920s and 1930s, an inveterate gambler be it in stocks and shares, foreign exchange markets, tin-pot gold mines or, most of all, horseracing. Bloodstock breeder, owner of a string of horses and steward of the Jockey Club, racing was a huge part of his life and, addicted to the adrenaline-packed excitement of the betting ring, he was a familiar figure with his glamorous wife at the Newmarket sales and Britain's most fashionable meetings. He was also one of the leading lights in a consortium to establish a new racecourse, Ensbury Park, on a former aerodrome near Bournemouth. Ensbury survived for three years until, like so many of his investments, it turned into an expensive failure and the land was sold for housing. All he had to show for it was his name in one of the roads, Broughton Avenue.

Delves Broughton's greatest racing success, and certainly the most controversial, occurred in 1927 when his Knight of the Grail won the Irish Derby, a victory that landed him in the civil courts where it was alleged he had reneged on an agreement to pay the previous owner £500 if the horse went on to win the big race. Dublin High Court entered judgement against him for £600, but, typical of his high-handed attitude, he refused to settle the matter and long after selling the horse, "cheaply" according to records, the case returned to court and he was additionally sued for libel. At the time he was a Deputy Lord Lieutenant of Cheshire, a magistrate and about to be appointed chairman of the Nantwich Bench. The truth, someone said of him, was often a stranger and he was prepared not merely to bend the rules but to see them tied in a Gordian knot.

Often absurdly self-important, vain and overbearing with a

Jock and Vera were familiar figures at major horseracing events.

haw-haw voice and what appeared to be a permanent unpleasant smell under his nose, Delves Broughton does not come across the years as a likeable man and, though popular with his workforce and tenants, his milieu was definitely amongst the privileged elite and, as evidenced by one notable fox-hunting incident, definitely not the hoi polloi. Riding with hounds his mount was kicked by a young farmer's horse and, without more ado, Delves Broughton hit the offending animal with the butt-end of his heavy hunting whip and pole-axed it to the ground. "That will teach you to come out on a kicker," he sneered at the young farmer.

By now Delves Broughton, the Great Gatsby of Cheshire, was flaunting his wealth on a vast scale, almost as if trying to buy all the fun and amusement he felt he had been deprived of in the past. At his London house prior to Ascot races there were great parties often attended by the Prince of Wales and Mrs Simpson, whilst the shooting weekends at Doddington Hall were the talk of society as he

Delves Broughton's Knight of the Grail wins the Duchess of York Plate at Hurst Park in 1927.

would hire an entire railway carriage to convey his guests from the capital to Crewe and, to while away the journey, they would quaff his champagne to the strains of his hired jazz band. The grand country house parties and the great shoots became part of Doddington Hall's fabric as much as Delves Broughton's penchant for disappearing into the bracken with titled ladies.

Once asked what was the most he had ever spent in a single year, he replied: "In a good year – 1926 I think – I spent £120,000. The first eighty was quite easy, but unless you gamble, the rest is sheer extravagance." £120,000 in 1926 is equivalent to just short of £5 million at current values.

It couldn't last and it didn't. Fifteen years of profligacy was catching up fast and, echoing Lord Delamere's predicament at Vale Royal although for vastly different reasons, he was unable to keep pace without selling off ever more of the Doddington estate to convert into cash in order to maintain his hugely expensive lifestyle and cover sustained gambling and investment losses. It was said he disposed of around 32,000 acres of Cheshire farmland and personally pocketed well over £1 million that should have

Weekends at Doddington Hall were famous. Here Jock Delves Broughton's son Evelyn rides out with Ava Baird, daughter of Lord Stonehaven.

been channelled into the family trust.

To further exacerbate the situation, his marriage was in deep trouble. Lady Vera was spending long periods away from home, cruising and African hunting in the company of Walter Guinness, Lord Moyne. Outwardly Jock Delves Broughton maintained an aura of indifference and when he wasn't fox-hunting, attending race meetings, or visiting his London clubs – The Guards and The Turf – he found himself rattling around Doddington Hall, bored and lonely, a disillusioned, morose figure, world weary and unable to build a relationship even with his son and heir, Evelyn, whom he treated with the same meanness he had suffered at the hands of his own father.

Jock Delves Broughton (left) with Lord Porchester.

One who knew Delves Broughton as well as anybody was Lord Porchester, the 6th Earl of Carnarvon, of Highclere Castle, who interviewed for the *White Mischief* book remarked: "Up at Doddington he'd lived high, wide and handsome. He'd betted and lost. And what's more, what he did was very dishonest. He'd rather make £10 crookedly than £100 straight. He, unbeknownst to Vera and the children, sold property and pictures which did not belong to him, which he'd no right to sell. Jock was perhaps a little vain and I think damn stupid if you ask me."

11

Father Christmas

IT was during one of Lady Vera's absences that Delves Broughton met Diana Caldwell, an alluring twenty-two-years-old platinum blonde, one of the adventurous liberated girls of the age. Full of vitality and sexually hypnotic she worked as a model in a London fashion house and during the evenings was a partner and hostess at Berkeley Square's Blue Goose cocktail club, a popular haunt for actors, actresses and the Bright Young Things, and known far and wide as a hunting ground for rich husbands.

Diana, model and hostess.

A fine horsewoman, Diana was also a regular guest at country houses sporting weekends and at one of these she fell in with thirty years older Jock Delves Broughton. The moment was summed up by journalist Cyril Connolly in a *Sunday Times*' magazine feature: "One day in 1935 he met his fate, his Green Hat, his Blue Angel, the woman who would renew his youth, bring him back into the world of feeling and set the death-wish ticking on a six-year fuse..."

Men drooled over Diana when she walked into a room. She oozed hormonal magnetism and, turning heads and hearts with equal ease, she soon had Delves Broughton so wrapped around her proverbial little finger that he bought her a flat in London's

The Bystander magazine: “Another ex-debutante who is seen around often is Diana Caldwell....”

Shepherd Street, his ego massaged by photographs of her appearing in society magazines.

Born in 1913, in Hove, Sussex, Diana was the second daughter of reasonably well-off Josiah Seymour Caldwell and between the ages of nine and seventeen she was educated at a private girls' school where her elder sister, Daphne, who went on to marry the Marquess of Willingdon, was also a boarder. Diana was no academic as one of her fellow students noted: “She was a games girl at school and a games girl for the rest of her life, but she was good fun and popular.” Her father doted on her and for her twentieth birthday in 1933 he gave her an open-top sports car. Locks flowing in the wind the former society debutante was on her way and a string of relationships followed.

Of course, Delves Broughton knew he was never likely to be the only man in her life, but he was besotted, at least until she fell pregnant with Vernon Motion, a tall, slim and good looking playboy pianist, mechanical engineer and pilot. Motion's sole claim to fame was a much-publicised 10,000 miles return business flight from England to Africa, a ground-breaking journey on which he was accompanied by a young female co-pilot, Frances Tollemache, who had managed to secure a flying licence from just three weeks' training. Incidentally, Frances's grandfather was Cheshire's largest landowner, eccentric Lord John Tollemache, the builder of Peckforton Castle near Tarporley.

Jock, besotted with Diana.

Vernon Motion may have been as promiscuous as Diana when they married at Chelsea Register Office and she immediately moved him into her Shepherd Street flat, much to the understandable chagrin of Delves Broughton. A mixed blessing, Diana miscarried and divorced Motion on the grounds of his adultery. It's possible, and certainly cannot be ruled out, that Delves Broughton was responsible for Diana's pregnancy and to avoid a scandal he paid Motion to take the rap, an aristocratic ploy not uncommon in those days and one certainly adopted by a well-known Tarporley Hunt Club contemporary to overcome a similar "difficulty".

Lady Vera Delves Broughton.

Pregnancy and divorce focused Diana's attention. Hand-to-mouth nonentities were best consigned to the flappers and, henceforth, Delves Broughton became her principal suitor, even if he was, as she confided in a friend, "as old as Father Christmas". Titled and seemingly a man of great wealth with a mansion and a country estate he appeared a good catch as she skipped along at his side, whilst he dragged behind him a portmanteau of memories.

Diana loved money and titles and, as long as he was financing her extravagances, she could not have cared less he was cheating his family trust and selling off his inheritance. So, during Lady Vera's many absences, she started living it up at Doddington Hall for the parties and hunting, the virtual wife. No-one was fooled, least of all Vera herself. More interested in furthering her own relationship with Lord Moyne, she looked with disdain on Diana and classed her as nothing more than a floosie, the latest of Jock's expensive passing fancies, and there had certainly been a few. Another who did not take kindly to Diana was Evelyn, Delves Broughton's son, who was barely a couple of years younger and despised her so much he persuaded a groom to corn up her horse before she went riding. Sure enough the horse bolted sharply and, most unlady like, Diana landed in a haystack much to the amusement of Evelyn.

Still, all the men considered her a goddess on a horse. "She looked absolutely stunning," remarked one of Evelyn's friends. "The most beautiful girl I had ever seen in the hunting field. She rode astride which was unusual in those days, and was always beautifully turned out and mounted, thanks to Jock."

In 1938 Britain was awash with rumours of war until Prime Minister Neville Chamberlain returned from Munich with his ill-fated "Peace in our time" pronouncement and, reflecting the changed national mood, Delves Broughton and Lady Vera were buoyed by relief and optimism when they made their final public appearance together at the wedding of their daughter, Rosamund, to Lord Lovat, the immensely rich laird of Beaufort Castle in Scotland. The reception was held at Lord Moyne's London home and Lady Vera had extra reason for optimism as he had recently become a widower. Only one obstacle, Jock, now stood in her way and she engaged a private detective to trail him to Liverpool's Adelphi Hotel where he stayed with an unnamed woman, presumably Diana.

Lady Vera did eventually get her divorce, but what a hypocrite. A big-game hunter and insatiable explorer she had accompanied Lord Moyne on many far-flung expeditions, one being a six-month trip covering 30,000 miles of Burma, China, New Guinea and Australia. She was also an accomplished photographer and provided the illustrations for his 1930s' books, *Atlantic Circle* and *Walkabout: A Journey in Lands Between the Pacific and Indian Oceans.*

Lady Vera lives it up
with Lord Moyne

There was certainly plenty of evidence for Delves Broughton to have commenced divorce proceedings on the other foot, but, of course, a gentleman seldom did in those days as it was a tacit admission of failure to keep a wife satisfied. Sadly for Lady Vera, she never married Lord Moyne as, in the midst of world war, he was assassinated whilst serving as Britain's Minister of State in Cairo. And thereby hangs a further twist in the Kenyan murder of Lord Erroll.

In Britain the ever-darkening war clouds were once more on the horizon in early 1939, not that they seemed to bother Delves Broughton who continued his upper-class existence. In February he was a distinguished guest with the Duke of Westminster and Lord Daresbury at the Cheshire Hunt Ball staged at the Grosvenor Hotel in Chester, and then it was on to his personal Grand National luncheon party, a hugely expensive annual gathering he financed for over one hundred guests at the Adelphi Hotel. All the food was cooked and prepared at Doddington Hall. Interlaced with the social whirl was the horseracing at venues such as Leopardstown, Newmarket, Chester and the local country course at Tarporley where Delves Broughton was a steward. His personal guests there included Tom Cholmondeley, the 4th Lord Delamere of Vale Royal.

What no-one could possibly have foreseen in the Spring sunshine of 1939 was that this would turn out to be the last ever meeting at Tarporley, or that within a few months, the winning jockey of the final race, Mr Luke Lillington, who had caused a stir by arriving on the racecourse in his own aeroplane, would be one of the first RAF pilots to perish in the Second World War.

12
Garden of Eden

Josslyn Victor Hay,
aka Joss Erroll

OLD Etonians, rarefied members of the British and Anglo-Irish society were amongst the new settlers to Kenya in the 1920s and one of the first was Josslyn Victor Hay, known to all as Joss Erroll, eldest son and heir of the 21st Earl of Erroll, of Slains Castle, Aberdeen. Brilliantly handsome with chiselled good looks, charm and arrogance in spades, Joss Erroll was a serial womaniser, a philanderer who specialised in bedding married women. His lair was the so-called "Happy Valley" region, beautiful highland farming country approximately one hundred miles north west of Nairobi where the meandering Wanjohi River was said to flow with champagne. Brilliantly handsome and imbued with an unassailable sense of his own superiority, Erroll was the "King Stud" of Happy Valley and he pursued women in the way other men hunted lion, his mantra "to hell with husbands". He had first made his name as a Lothario at the tender age of fifteen when he was expelled in disgrace from Eton for bonking with a housemaid twice his age and in 1924, causing his father to explode with rage, he scandalised society by marrying Lady Idina Sackville, a twice-divorced older woman who financed their escape

Joss Erroll and Lady Idina.

to Kenya where Lord Delamere greatly influenced him to take up farming and, in due course, politics. On the death of his father in 1928, Joss became the 22nd Earl of Erroll, Baron Kilmarnock and Lord High Constable of Scotland, an hereditary office bestowed on his family by Robert the Bruce.

Lady Idina and Joss Erroll were amongst several dozen English, Scots and Anglo-Irish silver-spooners, well-bred adventurers and gamblers seeking to create a private paradise, a life of pleasure and weapons-grade hedonism a long way from high taxes and dark Satanic mills of Britain. And within this pastoral idyll emerged the notorious Happy Valley set, a small clique of colonials who turned to drink, drugs and sexual promiscuity. Wives and husbands were swapped like cards in a game of gin rummy and just about every kind of carnal appetite was catered for and tolerated. Scandal in this steamy, tropical atmosphere was so commonplace as to rarely rate more than a bored yawn and, perhaps, the reality was far less exotic than has been handed down. Elspeth Huxley wrote: "Gin-soaked as they were, they enhanced rather than damaged the natural charms of their valley by leaving the native trees alone and creating gardens of outstanding beauty, by paddocking green pastures for butter-yellow Guernseys, stocking stream with trout and building attractive, rambling, creeper-festooned bungalows of local timbers with shingle roofs."

Lady Idina, a daughter of the 8th Earl De La Warr, was the undisputed presiding goddess, the ring mistress, often lying naked in a green onyx bath to welcome guests to cocaine-fuelled wife-swapping parties, her bedroom known enigmatically as the "Battlefield". Inevitably Idina and Joss divorced, not because of his other women or her sexual predilections but because he was cheating on her financially.

This portrait of Lady Idina, by the artist Sir William Orpen, sold for £1 million at Sotheby's of London in 2013.

Lady Idina went on to drift through a full hand of five husbands and in the process became a social pariah, her story told in a remarkable book *The Bolter,* written by her great-granddaughter Frances Osborne, the wife of Britain's former wallet-shaking Chancellor of the Exchequer, George Osborne, one-time MP for Tatton.

Women were attracted to

Joss Erroll like moths to a flame and he certainly played the field, although a rich wife was an absolute necessity to maintain his lifestyle and he soon married one of his lovers, Molly Ramsay-Hill, heiress to the Boots stores' fortune, but not before her rancher husband gave him a very public horse-whipping outside Nairobi railway station and then successfully claimed £3,000 damages to pay debts the pair had run up in his name. The judge denounced the Lord High Constable of Scotland a "very bad blackguard" and Molly no better. Many would have crawled away at such humiliation, but not Joss Erroll who journeyed to England by flying boat to undertake his very public ceremonial duty at the 1937 coronation of King George VI in Westminster Abbey. Two years later, and regardless of once being harnessed with thousands of others to the right-wing politics of the firebrand orator Sir Oswald Mosley, he was appointed to the wartime post of Assistant Military Secretary of East Africa, a glamorous adjunct to his already dashing persona.

Meanwhile, Molly was providing him with a generous income of £8,000 a year and also their beautiful lakeside Moroccan-style castle, Oserian, and it was here in 1939 she died of drink and drugs whilst he was out "philandering". Afterwards, down to his family pearls and unable to finance the upkeep of Oserian, he just happened to be casting around for a third wealthy spouse at the very moment Jock Delves Broughton arrived in Nairobi with his irresistible young wife Diana.

Amongst Erroll's friends were the Carberrys who had settled to farm a coffee plantation. John Carberry was a man with such a pathological hatred of England and before settling in Kenya he had dropped his title, 10th Baron Carbery, and sold his estates in Ireland. In modern parlance he was a nasty piece of work, a sadist who tortured animals and whipped his daughter. His third wife, June, was described as a "terrifying unnatural blonde, warm-hearted but tough as boots" and with a voice like a corncrake. Years later her stepdaughter, Juanita Carberry, went further: "She was a Piccadilly whore off the streets of London – she was a sexpot".

Alcohol and drug-fuelled wild parties were virtually a prerequisite for any who wished to embrace the Happy Valley social whirl and Juanita Carberry had a ringside view of the goings-on: "It was my destiny to grow up among a small group of people whose reputation for behaving badly has earned them a place in the history of colonialism. The Happy Valley set was a unique phenomenon. Shallow, spoiled and self-centred they were by nature metropolitan consumers who, set down in the Garden of Eden, found it dull. Many became addicts, either of drink or drugs. The people who built the colony were very different. They were doughty, decent men and women who earned their sundowners by the sweat of their brows."

American heiress
Alice de Janzé.

Others of the elite who swept in on the Lunatic Express included Alice Silverthorne, a $multi-million American heiress, who stumbled into the cauldron with her husband, Count Frédéric de Janzé, a French motor-racing ace and heir to an old aristocratic family in Brittany. The Count observed: "In this décor live a restless crowd of humans... hardly colonists, wanderers perhaps – indefatigable amusement seekers weary, or cast out from many climes, many countries. Misfits, neurasthenics, of great breeding and charm, who lack the courage to grow old, the stamina to pull up and build anew in this land."

The de Janzés found the atmosphere intoxicating and they too struck up a friendship with Lord Delamere who persuaded them to purchase a farm and predictably, as day follows night, Erroll had a fling with Alice, although it didn't last long as she suddenly fell madly in love with the latest to join the capricious Happy Valley band, Raymond Vincent de Trafford, whose once debt-ridden father, Sir Humphrey, the 3rd Baronet de Trafford, had landed a fortune by selling his English family seat, Trafford Hall, bordering on the then recently-opened Manchester Ship Canal. With 1,800 acres of land this came to be transformed into Trafford Park, the world's first industrial estate and, of course, the Old Trafford sporting arenas of Manchester United FC and Lancashire County Cricket Club. The de Traffords had been prominent landowners for centuries in Lancashire and Cheshire and Raymond's father was a fellow Tarporley Hunt Club member with Lord Delamere. Indeed, from as early as 1799, eight de Traffords are recorded as belonging to this

Sir Humphrey, 3rd Baronet de Trafford, and
his son Raymond, on horseback.

exclusive cabal, including two of Raymond's great uncles who resided at Hartford Manor, near to Delamere's Vale Royal estate.

Raymond (Christened "Raymond" but he preferred to spell his name "Raymund") had grown up a typical pampered playboy younger son with money to burn. He did a stint as a lieutenant in the Coldstream Guards, but the higher echelons of society were far more appealing and he was frequently photographed at Ascot and Gleneagles, hunting with the Beaufort, or riding in amateur steeplechase races alongside Edward, Prince of Wales. A gambler and a cad who left a string of bleeding hearts on a global scale, he claimed to have been attracted to Kenya by the farming opportunities and big-game hunting, although in reality it was probably more to do with the decadent lifestyle and, soon, he was doing what pleased him the most – gambling, womanising and drinking.

For a while he was Joss Erroll's only rival as the Don Juan of Happy Valley and, during one of his sojourns to East Africa, the British writer Evelyn Waugh, a fellow guest at Lord Delamere's Soysambu Ranch, wrote of him: "Very nice but so BAD and he fights and fucks and gambles and gets disgustingly drunk all the time... He brought a sluttish girlfriend back to the house. He woke me up to tell me he had just rogered her, and her mother too."

De Trafford and his friend Michael Lafone were notorious and their behaviour prompted an infamous Happy Valley ditty:

There was a young girl of the Mau
Who said she didn't know how.
She went for a cycle with Raymond and Michael.
She knows all there is to know now.

De Trafford's reputation preceded him but it certainly didn't deter Alice de Janzé and an affair raged with the devilishly hand-

Raymond de Trafford (left) with the de Janzés and Lord Delamere in the late 1920s.

some and hopelessly indiscreet Englishman. The cuckold Count de Janzé prayed it would be no more than a casual liaison, but his wife had other ideas and she was determined to marry her lover. The de Janzé marriage was eventually annulled by the Pope on the astonishing grounds that the union, in spite of there being two daughters, had not been consummated! It was suggested the Pontiff's decision was made easier by a large brown envelope of cash.

The die was cast and tragedy awaited at a French railway station when Alice and Raymond de Trafford rendezvoused in Paris to discuss their forthcoming marriage. However, true to form, he had changed his mind, declaring that he was immediately leaving for England as his father, vehemently opposed to him marrying a divorcee, was threatening to disinherit him. Alice's pleas fell on deaf

Lord Delamere enjoys a lighter moment in his twilight years.

ears and as they said their farewells in the compartment of de Trafford's train at the Gare du Nord, she suddenly pulled out a pistol, pressed the muzzle into his chest and fired. She then shot herself in the stomach. Alice's wounds were superficial but for a while de Trafford's life hung by a thread – the bullet had missed his heart by a fraction.

The incident made sensational headlines across the world and nine months later, when they had both recovered, Alice stood trial in France, charged with assault, rather than attempted murder, her legal team successfully arguing that she had been mentally irresponsible at the time of the shooting. When asked why she took the gun to the railway station, Alice replied: "To kill myself and I nearly succeeded." De Trafford agreed: "As we were about to part – she was kissing me. I told her that I loved her and again whispered to her not to take my decision as irrevocable. I even told her we would meet again. As she was leaving she attempted suicide, but a movement on my part caused the weapon to be deflected. The accident was due to my imprudence."

Viewed by the French public as the tragic victim of a crime passionnel Alice got away with a suspended prison sentence and a fine of one-hundred francs, both subsequently annulled under a presidential pardon. For his part, de Trafford was rebuked by the court for his failure to deliver on his promise to marry her. Alice returned to Kenya but was immediately forced to leave the country as an undesirable alien and, unperturbed by her friends who could not understand her fixation with such a patently obnoxious man, she went in hot pursuit of her lover. The principal stumbling block to their marriage, Raymond's father, Baronet Humphrey, had died in 1932 and, finally, they married in the town hall of Neuilly, a wealthy suburb of Paris. Within two months Alice was filing for a legal separation and, to be rid of him, she paid his first-class passage to Australia. Their marriage had lasted three weeks.

As the wife of a British subject Alice was allowed to return to Kenya and, though de Trafford briefly attempted to revive their relationship, she became involved in yet another scandal when a newspaper reporter caught her making love to Oswald Mosley.

Near broke Raymond de Trafford returned to England and finished up in prison as, under the influence of alcohol, he had killed a woman cyclist whilst driving home from a race meeting at Cheltenham. Found guilty of manslaughter he was sentenced to three years, appearing on Maidstone Prison's 1939 electoral roll as being of "independent means – retired". On his release he declared himself bankrupt.

Whilst incarcerated at Maidstone he would have heard of Joss Erroll's murder in Kenya and, also, that his niece, a daughter of the 4th Baronet de Trafford, had given birth to a son, Andrew Parker Bowles, who would go on to become the first husband of Camilla, Duchess of Cornwall.

13

Castle of Tears

DELAMERE and Delves Broughton are names chiselled into the story of Kenya. Another is Egerton, Maurice Egerton, the fourth and last Baron Egerton of Tatton, a man apart who, spurned in love, left two remarkable legacies to Britain and Kenya.

Lord Maurice Egerton.

When Maurice Egerton was born, in 1874, his family had been settled at Knutsford since the 16th century and surrounded by thousands of acres of gardens and a deer park opulent Tatton Hall was one of the wonders of Cheshire, heaving with rare paintings, china and elegant furnishings.

Educated at Eton and the Royal Agricultural College, Maurice Egerton excelled in zoology and veterinary science and became fascinated with the technical discoveries of the age, especially aviation. One of the earliest British pioneers to acquire a pilot's licence he had his own plane and landing strip at Tatton and, friendly with Wilbur and Orville Wright, he attained the rank of Major in the newly-formed Royal Air Force. Big-game hunting, radio transmission, photography and automobiles were amongst many diverse interests and his 24hp Darracq motor car was the first vehicle in Cheshire to be allocated a registration number, M1

On succeeding his father in 1920 and as the new Lord Egerton he travelled to Kenya and became another inspired by Lord Delamere, his great friend from Eton and the Tarporley Hunt Club. Egerton was allotted land by the British government in the Nakuru-Njoro region and this he added to when Delamere, ever in financial difficulty, sold him a further 21,000 acres. Possessed of enormous wealth coupled with exceptional inventive and technical skill, he immersed himself in Kenya as a successful farmer developing sisal, tea and coffee plantations. He also invested heavily in native industries and, like Delamere, though even more of a loner, he was far removed from the shenanigans of the Happy Valley set.

Smaller than the butler's pantry at Tatton and reminiscent of Delamere's own early days, Egerton's first home was a rudimentary grass-roofed structure that served him well until, in his sixties, he built himself a more substantial four-roomed cottage to impress a high-born young Austrian lady whom he was determined to make his wife. She took one look, remarked that it resembled a chicken

Egerton and a 1900 Benz displaying
Cheshire's first registration number, M1.

Tatton Hall, the ancestral home of Lord Egerton.

coop, and flounced off back to Europe. Faint heart never won fair lady and he responded by embarking on creating a colossally expensive new house, Egerton Castle, a fairytale palace in Africa fit for a princess.

Unfortunately, due to the Second World War and his return to Tatton for the duration, it took him fifteen years to complete the magnificent four-storey edifice, a scaled down version of Tatton Hall designed by an English architect. The finest materials from Europe and the Orient were used and the completed work included fifty-two magnificent rooms, an enormous ballroom, library, elevator, photographic studio, guesthouses and servants' quarters. Alas, the errant lady remained unimpressed and, declaring the castle a monument to vanity, she left him for good, this time to marry an Austrian nobleman.

Embittered and downcast in his castle of tears Egerton, no family, no heirs, no incentive to preserve his worldly goods, receded into a fantasy world, a lonely old man with a pathological hatred of women whom he threatened to shoot if any dared cross his

Egerton's fairytale castle in Kenya.

threshold, an edict extended to visiting friends' wives and daughters who were ordered to stay eight miles away. He died at the age of eighty-three and his name, to this day, is revered in Kenya in consequence of him having given 740 acres of land to start an agricultural school. It was, he said, a memorial to Lord Delamere, a truth that has long been buried.

On his death in 1958, Egerton left the castle and a further 1,100 acres to the school and this is now Egerton University, the country's oldest institution of higher education. In England the Egerton Barony became extinct and Tatton Hall with its parkland was bequeathed to the National Trust, "to be preserved for the benefit of the nation".

Lord Maurice Egerton's cousin, the 9th Earl Albemarle, wrote of him: "He was of a kind and generous bent, interested in fellow beings, particularly the young, yet the whole appearance was marred by the desire of keeping himself to himself, yet when he was amongst friends he gave many smiles and good fellowship, and was capable of thoroughly enjoying himself."

14

Are you married or do you live in Kenya?

August 1939: The world holds its breath as Hitler's troops mass on the Polish border. On the other side of Europe war seems a million miles away as Diana Caldwell holidays with rich friends on the Cote d'Azur, a jolly financed by her lover Jock Delves Broughton. She has with her his latest gift, the Broughton Pearls, and whilst she dines in Cannes the necklace is mysteriously snatched from her car. Delves Broughton duly claims the insurance. Two months pass and three valuable paintings are stolen from Doddington Hall, the insurance company once again pays out handsomely. Years later an associate confesses he had been enlisted by the late Sir Jock to stage both scams. The paintings were thrown into a local canal, the Broughton Pearls concealed at Doddington Hall.

BY 1940 there wasn't a lot going for Jock Delves Broughton apart from Diana who was, to his mind, "playing silly war games" as an itinerant ambulance driver in bomb-blitzed London. The true love of his life, Lady Vera, was about to be granted her decree absolute, he'd critically eroded the family trust, insurance investigators were on his trail over the pearls and Doddington Hall was about to be commandeered for the war effort. Nor could the international situation have been much worse as Britain teetered on the verge of invasion following the fall of Denmark, Holland and France.

As the Irish Guards' survivor had remarked in the First World

Diana the temptress.

War, Delves Broughton wasn't a "very bellicose gent" and in 1940 he unpatriotically decided to quit and make another run for it, this time to Kenya where his coffee plantation seemed an infinitely more pleasant place to sit out the conflict's horrors. With little money, few real prospects and nothing to lose, Diana was easily persuaded to fall in with the plan in spite of understandable misgivings about the potentially perilous journey ahead of them.

Securing a wartime passage was no easy matter for mere mortals, but, with the advantage of the old boys' network, Delves Broughton managed to arrange berths on one of the last ships to carry passengers to South Africa, the staging post for Kenya. Diana travelled as his secretary and as their ship zig-zagged to avoid

German U-boats he spent much of the voyage playing bridge whilst she slept with other men. The detritus of war, their arrival in South Africa coincided with the legal rubber-stamping of Lady Vera's divorce and, for better or worse, Jock and Diana exchanged vows in Durban on November 5. If he wanted fireworks he was about to get them.

Diana may not have had the slightest reservation about being a kept woman, but she had no intention of saddling herself with "Father Christmas" and before they tied the knot she insisted on him committing to a prenuptial legal agreement. If she was to fall in love with a younger man there would be no recriminations, or hard feelings, and, crucially, he would agree to a divorce and give her £5,000 annually for seven years. It was laughable. As his will was later to show, he could hardly have mustered the first downpayment without raiding the family trust.

Diana was delighted, not only in grasping the title and access to perceived wealth, but also an escape route whenever it took her fancy. For his part, Delves Broughton entered into the marriage and prenup fully aware his bride attracted men like bees to a honeypot, her past and present littered with affairs. But, for the moment, he wasn't overly concerned about the consequences and in a sense he was putting two fingers up to his ex-wife. He would dazzle Nairobi society with Vera's ravishing replacement and be the envy of them all. What a coup for his over-inflated ego even though a friend had warned him before they left England that every man was going to fall for Diana – "Oh, that's all right," he responded gullibly. "I'm not the least bit jealous." It was bravado he would quickly regret as since his last visit there was a new colonial dynamic, the three As – "Attitude, Alcohol and Adultery", or as the quip went: "Are you married or do you live in Kenya?"

When they reached Nairobi the Delves Broughtons immediately made for the Muthaiga Club, chief watering hole of the Happy

Valley set, to lunch with Jock's acquaintance of many years, Gwladys Lady Delamere. Diana took the opportunity to emphasise her elevated status by firing off several postcards, one addressed to the caretaker at Doddington Hall: "I used to get cards from Miss Caldwell asking after the dogs," he said. "They were always signed Diana Caldwell. Then one came signed Lady Broughton."

*****

Staid and sometimes embarrassingly out of place in Nairobi, Delves Broughton seldom missed an opportunity to display his effervescent trophy wife, regardless of what the gossips were saying, that she'd only married "Poor old Jock" for his money and title. It was , of course, perfectly true and intoxicated by the new lifestyle, Diana stylishly brazened it out by literally gate-crashing the round of endless parties and dances, Delves Broughton allowing her the freedom to attend without him. "One must keep a young wife amused," he would say tolerantly.

Inevitably delectable Diana, twenty-seven, caught the eye of Kenya's lecherous lord, thirty-nine years old Joss Erroll and, as recounted by a Nairobi bandleader, they were soon dancing as close as "two sardines", she wearing a skin-tight long dress that showed every part of her wonderful body. As they passed the band she asked him to play a tune for them – "Let's fall in love".

And fall in love they did as an affair began to rage for all to see. Delves Broughton must have realised what was going on and yet it didn't seem to bother him. He had known Erroll for years and got on well with him, kindred spirits, both panting for money but trapped in the murky world of family trusts. Indeed he remained sanguine when Gwladys Lady Delamere took it upon herself to spell out the depth of Diana's behaviour. Mocking notes then began to appear for

Joss Erroll, the lecherous lord.

Delves Broughton at the Muthaiga Club: January 6, 1941 – "You seemed like a cat on hot bricks at the club last night. What about the eternal triangle? What are you going to do about it?"; January 18 – "Do you know your wife and Lord Erroll have been staying alone at the Carberrys' house in Nyeri together?"; January 21 – "There's no fool like an old fool. What are you going to do about it?"

A proud man pitchforked aside, Delves Broughton was reduced to brooding impotence, a laughing stock, and he made an official complaint to the police about the notes. The writer was never identified but the Happy Valleyers were sure it was the work of Gwladys Lady Delamere who frequently caroused at the Muthaiga Club although she was never part of the decadent in-crowd.

She'd once had a brief fling with Erroll and, in spite of his never-ending dalliances with younger and prettier women, she still adored him. However the interloper Diana was upsetting the delicate balance of Nairobi's capricious coterie and she was probably deeply jealous. Surrounded by innuendo and wagging tongues, Delves Broughton, the racing man and gambler, started to realise it might be time to cut his losses and he talked of moving to Ceylon (Sri Lanka) and he asked Diana to accompany him there for a preliminary extended holiday, to give her time to get over Erroll.

Diana pointblank refused and in that case, he told her, he would commence divorce proceedings. Their marriage, if it could be called "marriage", had lasted barely eleven weeks and though they were living under the same roof – she once described him as a "dirty old man" – it's doubtful they had ever shared a bed in Kenya.

Delves Broughton pressed on with his plan to move to Ceylon and to all appearances he was handling his humiliating loss with gallant magnanimity. He later recalled, "I loved her in spite of everything and I hoped that all might still come right in the end."

Two days before his scheduled departure, in January 1941, he organised a farewell dinner at the Muthaiga Club with Diana, Erroll and his houseguest June Carberry making up an odd foursome. As the evening drew to a close he proposed a most bizarre toast under the circumstances:

'To Diana and Joss I wish them every happiness and may their union be blessed with an heir. To Diana and Joss and their future heir." For a moment Diana, Joss and June sat in stunned silence and then with a nervous laugh continued to sip their champagne. Soon afterwards as the lovers prepared to leave the restaurant to go dancing, Delves Broughton, acting more like a protective father than

The Delves Broughtons' house in Marula Lane, Karen.

an abandoned husband, asked Erroll to make sure Diana was safely home by 3am. In fact, it was shortly before 2.30am when they got back to the house at Karen. The housekeeper, Dorothy Wilks, let them in, Delves Broughton and June Carberry, both apparently worse the wear for drink, had already retired to their bedrooms. All appeared quiet as Erroll drove off into the night and Diana joined June Carberry in her bed.

Approximately a quarter of an hour later, according to police timings, two dairy workers driving in the drizzle on the main Karen to Nairobi road came across an arc of bright light from a car's head-lamps. There seemed to have been some sort of accident and the men tentatively approached the vehicle, a large Buick. Its nose was sunk into a shallow murram (gravel) pit and when they peered inside they saw the body of a white man, a soldier in military uniform, slumped in the footwell, blood seeping from a head wound. He was obviously dead and by dawn, the scene crawling with police officers, it soon became apparent the body was that of Lord Erroll, the Assistant Military Secretary. Two shots had been fired from a .32 calibre revolver, the fatal bullet entering his brain by the side of the left ear. The biggest scandal ever to hit Kenya was about to unfold.

At first Nairobi police tried to keep a lid on the fact they were dealing with murder and, by the following morning, British and Kenyan newspapers were reporting Erroll had died in a motor accident. Three days later, with full military honours, Nairobi's most famous citizen was laid to rest in a small cemetery next to the grave of his second wife Molly. The mourners included Kenya's Governor, Commissioner of Police, military representatives, senior heads of government departments, members of the Legislative Council and friends from all walks of life. Jock Delves Broughton arrived late, but Erroll's last lover, Diana, did not attend.

The *East African Standard* reported: "Units of the South African

Forces provided the bearer party and the firing party. The latter lined the entrance to the cemetery and as the hearse bearing the coffin – draped with a Union Jack – approached, the party reversed arms and stood with bowed head as the cortege entered the gates. As the simple, but impressive service came to an end, the firing party loaded and three volleys were fired. Then the bugler sounded the Last Post."

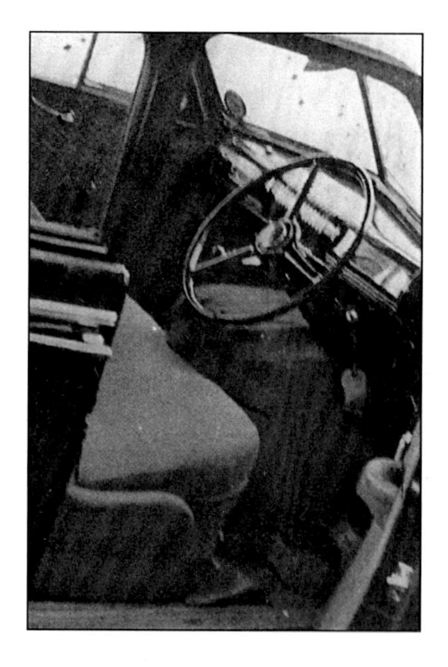

Erroll's body thrust into the Buick's footwell.

A former member of Scotland Yard's Flying Squad, Superintendent Arthur Poppy, was in charge of the murder investigation and he certainly had no easy task. There was a shortage of clues and, from the start, the crime scene at the road junction was an utter shambles. A proper examination of the body had not taken place and officers had trampled a possible second set of tyre tracks into the mud. Curiously, the Buick had not been fingerprinted before it was removed and throughly washed at a local garage. Some onlookers were actually allowed to sit inside the vehicle in which a mechanic discovered a woman's hairgrip and a cigarette-end, both stained with blood. There also a strong, lingering smell of perfume – hardly surprising given that most Happy Valley women, including Diana, habitually laced themselves with Chanel.

The lack of forensic evidence hampered Poppy as shockwaves reverberated through the privileged community at the thought of a killer in their midst, and to complicate matters there were numerous suspects, including a posse of cuckolded husbands who considered Erroll, the philandering swordsman of Happy Valley, a "first-rate shit". Other than that there was a wall of silence and Poppy's frustrations must have increased tenfold when he attempted to interview Erroll's redoubtable former wife, Lady Idina, at her home in the Aberdare mountains.

A servant directed him to a seat on the verandah and when Lady Idina eventually appeared she was smoking a cigarette in a long-necked holder and wearing high heels. Other than that she was stark naked. Sitting down beside him, she said: "Well, Sergeant Poppy, how can I help you?" Superintendent Poppy later admitted to colleagues it was the most difficult interview he had ever conducted in his entire police career.

Undeterred Poppy, or "Popski" as he was referred to by the Happy Valleyers, pressed on with the investigation and few were surprised when he homed in on Jock Delves Broughton who was charged with murder and remanded in custody to await trial. "You are making a big mistake," he told Poppy who was convinced of his guilt.

Delves Broughton's arrest sent the newspapers into frenzied overdrive, especially in Britain where an exciting interlude of sex, adultery and murder involving an English baronet and Scotland's foremost peer, fleetingly brightened the nation's wartime austerity. The magnitude of the situation reverberated across the world and nowhere was it felt more than in Haifa, Palestine, where four British army officers, all would-be members of the Tarporley Hunt Club, were settling down to Sunday lunch – Major Richard Verdin, of Stoke Hall, Nantwich; Major Sir Philip Lever, of Thornton Manor, Thornton Hough; Lt. Charles Brocklehurst, of Hare Hill, Macclesfield; and Capt. Michael Higgins, of Sandymere, Delamere.

Delves Broughton was one of their own and, according to Gordon Fergusson in his history of the Tarporley Hunt Club, Dickie Verdin, a budding barrister, was reading the Sunday edition of the *Palestine Post* when suddenly he exclaimed: "Good God! Jock's been charged with murder. I must go to Nairobi to defend him."

Being wartime Dickie was naturally refused leave to participate and Delves Broughton's counsel was to be spearheaded by flamboyant and aggressive Harry Morris, KC, who was known as the "Genius of the Defence". Said to be "bluff, rough, impassioned and contemptuous", he was a bruising cross-examiner, one of the finest advocates in South Africa, and it had been Diana who had engaged him whilst Delves Broughton languished in jail awaiting trial. She flew to Johannesburg to charm Morris and, attracted by the prestige of the case, he agreed. A daily bottle of whisky and a fee of £5,000 ensured his acceptance and, in due course, he became confident he would save Delves Broughton on one critical point of ballistics, though he adamantly refused to tell anyone, including his client, what the case-breaker would be.

15

Genius of the Defence

JOCK Delves Broughton's trial opened in Nairobi's Supreme Court on May 26, 1941 before an all-white jury of twelve farmers and businessmen. He was indicted for the murder of Captain the Right Honourable Josslyn Victor Hay, 22nd Earl of Erroll and Baron Kilmarnock, and for almost six weeks the courtroom was packed to the rafters with the cream of Kenyan society and international journalists all panting for every salacious detail of life, love and murder in Happy Valley. With Diana in the public gallery taking centre stage each day in a different, expensive new outfit, the case titillated and horrified war-torn Britain.

The Attorney General led for the Crown, the thrust of the case against Delves Broughton basically straightforward: Whilst Erroll was saying goodnight to Diana he had climbed down a drainpipe, hidden in the car and shot his love rival when they were out of sight of the house. He had then pushed Erroll's body away from the steering wheel, started the vehicle towards the ditch and walked home through the Bush, a shortcut of just over one mile. The Crown argued that Delves Broughton was a man of position used to getting exactly what he wanted and when faced with the break-up of his three months' marriage, robbed of his dearest possession, he had taken the law into his own hands. He was an arch-plotter who had lulled Lord Erroll into a false sense of security and then inveigled him to Karen to murder him.

Much was made of what Erroll had said to a friend shortly before his death: "Jock could not have been nicer. He has agreed to go away. As a matter of fact, he's been so nice it smells bad." And then there had been a conversation overheard in the Muthaiga Club after Erroll and Diana had left to go dancing on the fateful night. In an angry, raised voice Delves Broughton allegedly said to June Carberry: "I'm not going to give her £5,000 a year or the house at Karen. She can bloody well go and live with Joss."

Alternatively, June Carberry testified she had never known Delves Broughton to exhibit the slightest jealousy of Lord Erroll and, moreover, he was willing to do everything possible to enable him to marry Diana. She stated that Delves Broughton had twice looked in on her during the night, the last time at 3.30am, to make sure she was all right, and after Erroll's departure Diana had joined her for a bedroom chat. A strange witness, June Carberry later privately admitted she'd lied under oath, but which part of her evidence was false remains a mystery. Was she trying to protect Delves Broughton, or Diana, her alleged lesbian lover?

Hostile witness Gwladys.

Amongst thirty prosecution witnesses to take the stand, unquestionably the most hostile was Gwladys Lady Delamere, the provocative mayor of Nairobi who was a formidable adversary for even Harry Morris, Delves Broughton's celebrated QC. Etiquette amongst the Happy Valley set demanded a show of solidarity for Delves Broughton, but clearly Gwladys had it in for him and, to put it mildly, her evidence was blunt. At first she said she knew him well from her former marriage in England, but then immediately contradicted herself by dismissing him as a mere "acquaintance".

Asked by Morris what Erroll and

Diana's affair had to do with her, Lady Delamere responded: "Merely that I was an old friend of Lord Erroll's and I anticipated trouble and difficulties for all three." She went on to claim Delves Broughton had spoken of Diana in the most abusive terms and when she was dancing with Erroll his expression had registered "anger, misery, rage, brooding, intense agitation and restlessness". At the end of cross-examination Lady Delamere was asked by a member of the jury whether Delves Broughton was habitually "morose" as she had implied, or would the word "reserved" suit equally well. She refused to agree whereupon the juryman suggested it might be that Delves Broughton was only morose towards Lady Delamere. "If so," she snapped tartly, "he must have been morose for twenty years."

The Crown case appeared strong but with so much circumstantial evidence it was hardly impregnable and, furthermore, under English law, guilt had to be proved beyond reasonable doubt. Morris in his inimitable style set about dismantling the evidence piece by piece, starting with the fact there hadn't been a single eye-witness to any of it and, for good measure, he made mincemeat of the police and prosecution's interpretation of events, claiming that Delves Broughton had drunk excessively at the Muthaiga Club and, due to physical disabilities, was incapable of shinning down a drainpipe, or scurrying anywhere, let alone through the Bush in the blackness of the night.

Having already succeeded in turning several of the prosecution witnesses to testify to Delves Broughton's general amiability and tolerance, Morris cited the fact that in England in 1924, Delves Broughton had been before the Ministry of Pensions Board and was granted a forty percent disability certificate. He had a gammy leg, was prone to a certain amount of mental and physical tiredness and confusion, and with poor eyesight he suffered from night blindness. Morris also drew attention as to how Delves Broughton could possibly have got back into the house undetected when it was accepted the staircase creaked and groaned at every footfall. The Crown, he said, had not satisfactorily explained how the accused had managed to slip in and out of the house undetected. It was also of the utmost significance that not a speck of blood had been found on a single garment Delves Broughton had worn that night.

As an experienced magistrate in Cheshire acquainted with English law Delves Broughton must, surely, have appreciated there was a lack of substantive evidence and throughout five days on the stand he remained a calm, old school English gentleman appearing utterly guiltless as he repelled with majestic ease everything the Crown threw at him.

"Diana has never told me that she is in love with me but I am frightfully in love with her," he said. Their marriage had been blissful until she fell for Lord Erroll, but he'd become reconciled to the situation and had every intention of abiding by their pact, although he felt sure Diana would not have asked for the money. "You have to visualise the possibility of your wife falling in love with another man younger than yourself," he added. "My word was pledged and I could do nothing about it, but naturally it made me unhappy."

The Attorney General and the Chief Justice then pressed him to state whether it was flattering for another man to fall in love with his wife. "I think it is," responded Delves Broughton. "One always likes to see one's possessions admired." And was his pride hurt? "Not my pride. She was taken away by a much younger man, an intelligent man, a very attractive man, and a man of very high social position." Would that have made it more pleasant? "I think much more, my Lord."

He flatly denied having anything to do with Erroll's murder and when suggested this was a "very satisfactory solution" to his marital problems, he replied dryly: "I do not think that an average man would relish resuming married life with one who had been madly in love, and still is, with another man."

In regard to Lady Delamere's venomous evidence, he said: "Parts are correct and parts are very incorrect indeed. On our arrival in the country Lady Delamere not only had lunch with my wife and myself, but dined with us and treated me as a very old friend and told me I had never looked so happy. Now apparently she has taken to dislike me. This I fail to understand. When she was married to Lord Delamere I stayed up at Government House, Entebbe for a week and we played golf together and were most happy and amicable and the best of friends. Lord Delamere was almost my greatest friend out here and a near neighbour of mine in England. Nobody was more surprised than I was at her evidence. It was entirely fabricated."

Ultimately, the outcome of the trial hinged on ballistics and identification of the alleged murder weapon, a revolver the police claimed had been owned and suspiciously reported stolen by Delves Broughton a few days before Erroll's murder. This was the moment for Morris to show his hand and with trademark flourish he snatched the proverbial rug from under the entire Crown case. Firearms certificates issued by Cheshire Police in 1940 showed Delves Broughton's two revolvers were a Colt .32 and a Colt .45 and Morris proved both had six *anti*-clockwise rifling grooves. The murder bullet had come from an unidentified pistol with five clockwise grooves. It was a masterstroke and, as Morris had anticipated, the turning point.

In his summing up he maintained that the Crown had based its entire case on theory and speculation, seeking to prove a cold-blooded and carefully planned assassination, a depraved, diabolical and unspeakable offence. Yet, not at any time had Delves Broughton ever uttered one single threat against the life of Lord Erroll, nor had he shown the slightest resentment towards him. The Crown's every effort had failed to show Delves Broughton was of irritable disposition, likely to resort to violence, and it was ludicrous to suggest that because he had remained calm throughout his court ordeal it was due to a guilty conscience.

There was no evidence to prove he left the house, no evidence that he was absent or seen elsewhere, and the absence of blood on his clothes was of the utmost significance. The jury was being asked to believe that the accused had flung from himself the fumes of intoxicants to become clear-headed; that he was endowed with the agility of youth to climb out of the window; that despite his physical incapacity and his defective eyesight he had managed to shoot Erroll, bundle him into the footwell of the car and drive 2.4 miles to the road junction before walking across country back to his house.

It was utterly implausible. To convict Delves Broughton the jury had to be absolutely sure he had murdered Erroll and, as no-one could be sure, he had to be given the benefit of doubt. Morris, the "Genius of the Defence", certain throughout of his client's innocence, was not present to hear the spontaneous cheering and applause that greeted the "Not guilty" verdict, or notice the "thumbs-up" from Delves Broughton's barber who happened to be one of the jurymen.

16

I about to die salute thee

NO wonder, when he made his way out of the courtroom, Delves Broughton looked as if he'd backed a 100/1 winner. It had been the longest trial in Kenya records and, seldom faltering, he had answered over fifteen-hundred Crown questions and emerged from his ordeal with flying colours.

Declaring he'd never enjoyed himself so much in his life, he wrote to a friend: "Well, all's well that ends well but the fact remains that I was in jail for nearly four months which was a severe jolt to my well organized and happy life. It just shows how easy it is to get in trouble through no fault of your own… The Foreman in a clear voice said 'Not Guilty' and a loud sob of relief came from all over the court and a good deal of clapping. One could almost feel the Angel of Death who had been hovering over me, flying out of that court disgruntled. When I got outside there was a great rush of about 200 people headed by most of the Police to shake me by the hand. People have been extraordinarily kind and I have had 146 cables of congratulations and countless letters from all over the world, lots of them from people I've never heard of. I had practically the whole country solidly behind me from the start. I drove with some friends to a house where Diana was waiting for me. I did not let her come into court the last day. She, poor dear, had had a much worse time than I have. The wicked part is that it cost me £5,000 which I have not got and, of course, as the Crown can do no wrong, I can recover nothing. I got the best counsel in Africa – Morris of Johannesburg."

When he heard the verdict on his return to South Africa, Morris sent Delves Broughton a letter saying he had never doubted his innocence for a moment and congratulated him on his honesty and sincerity as a witness. Delves Broughton made a hundred copies of the letter and sent them to his friends who responded with their own congratulations, one of them the Earl of Carnarvon, Lord Porchester, a fellow horseracing doyen, who mischievously cabled: "Hearty congratulations – understand you won a neck cleverly. Regards Porchey." The acquittal also came as a great relief to the likes of Dickie Verdin et al in Palestine, and to members of the Tarporley Hunt Club in Cheshire.

There wasn't a scintilla of hard evidence to prove Delves Broughton murdered Erroll and, almost eighty years later, there still isn't despite the best efforts of many authors. In Kenya, however, the euphoria of acquittal was short-lived as searing doubts began to rankle amongst the Nairobi naysayers marshalled by Gwladys Lady Delamere who regarded the verdict a blatant miscarriage of justice. Delves Broughton may have been found not guilty, but he wasn't innocent enough and Gwladys Delamere stirred up the doubters by having him ostracised from the Muthaiga Club, the worst possible ignominy, although in that regard he was in good company as she had previously been instrumental, "Not British you know", in barring the Aga Khan.

Appearing not to give a damn that wartime Britain was on its knees, enduring the Blitz, food rationing and the threat of Nazi invasion, Delves Broughton's response to the wagging tongues and innuendo was to sail away with Diana who had finally agreed to holiday with him in Ceylon and India. When they got back to Kenya months later it seemed they might settle down together, but it was not to be as Diana instantly waltzed off to land another pushover, Gilbert de Preville Colville, who was twenty-five years older and had been at Eton at the same time as Delves Broughton.

A scruffy, taciturn odd-ball who lived a monk-like existence and seldom spoke to women he was, alongside glamorous Diana, a care-worn, wizened little man. Some said he was tight-fisted and probably the most boring man in the world, only ever interested in talking about cattle and rain, but. as far as concerned Diana. he was Kenya's richest and largest rancher, the "Beef Baron", able to offer her the greatest asset she craved more than anything... enormous wealth.

Delves Broughton's life went steadily downhill from the moment Diana walked away and, convinced she had wrecked his life he turned to drink, his craving worsened when he was thrown from his horse and had to be encased in plaster. Contradicting his court-room pronouncements that he had been blissfully happy with Diana, he disconsolately wrote to his solicitor in Nairobi: "This woman I married is about the worst in the way of female God ever put breath into. She had a violent affair with an Italian while she was engaged to me. She wrote a letter to the Italian from my own house saying 'I am longing to make love to you – desperately' etc. The copy of the letter is among my papers. She had a violent affair with an officer on the boat I took her out to Africa on. When we were in Durban she asked another man to come on honeymoon with us. Within two months of our marriage she had the violent affair with Erroll which ended with me being tried for murder. In December 1941 she contracted a very intensive friendship with Gilbert Colville. She told me he was the richest man in Kenya and that she would get him to leave her his money. She has gone on with this and has been completely successful. In the early part of July this year I twice caught her in bed with a soldier – she has hunted me like a dog all the time."

With nothing left to keep him in Kenya, Delves Broughton waited in Mombasa for a troopship to take him back to England, a hazardous passage via Cape Town, and during the voyage he sarcastically cabled Gilbert Colville with a cutting reference to Erroll's former home, Oserian, which was up for sale: "You've got the bitch.

Now buy her the kennel." It was precisely two years since he had travelled in the opposite direction with Diana and, bitterly, he wrote to her: "I am determined to punish you for ruining my life in the way you have done."

Downcast and pain-wracked from his spinal injury throughout the sea voyage, he was at the end of his tether when his ship docked in Liverpool and matters were soon to plummet further when he was met, probably acting on a tip-off from the Kenyan police, by two Scotland Yard detectives wanting to question him about the theft of the Broughton pearls. The interview had a crushing effect on Delves Broughton and on his return to Doddington, the hall being used as a wartime school, he stayed on the far side of the park with his faithful butler Frank Martin. Few amongst his neighbours and friends were aware he was home and for the best part of a fortnight he wandered the grounds, a sorrowful figure engrossed in the unholy mess in which he found himself. Persona non grata in Kenya, Diana had ditched him, his finances were at a critically low ebb, the police had their teeth in over the pearls and his ex-wife Vera had categorically refused to take him back. Tragedy was in the making and Wednesday December 2, 1942 marked the start of a shattering climax.

On that morning Delves Broughton instructed his chauffeur, Cartwright, to take him into Nantwich, to a solicitor's office where he was to sign and complete the formalities of his personal will. Giving his address as Frank Martin's Badgers Bank Farm at Hatherton, the document was pathetically brief for a man of Delves Broughton's high-standing, hardly more than three-hundred words. He left his daughter, Rosamund Lady Lovat, "any little trinket she may desire", to his son, Evelyn, a gold cigarette case, a gold watch and a twelve-bore shotgun "...and nothing else as he is amply provided for". His former valet, the ever-loyal Charles Pegram, was to receive 300 guineas, Frank Martin £100 and bedroom furniture, and Thomas Frost, of London, all his cigars "as I know he is fond of them". Chauffer Cartwright and the solicitor's clerk formally witnessed his signature and within a few minutes he was on his way to Crewe Station to board a Liverpool-bound train.

Ostensibly the purpose of the journey was to prepare for the removal of his back plaster at Liverpool's Northern Hospital and he had booked himself into one of his favourite haunts, the Adelphi Hotel, where he had lavishly entertained Grand National guests in those balmy days before the war. Poignantly it was also where he had taken Diana, the likely "unnamed woman" cited in Vera's divorce proceedings.

During the afternoon of his arrival, he informed the Adelphi head housekeeper that, under no circumstances, was he to be disturbed until Sunday. The maids were not to make his bed and as to meals he insisted he would be looking after himself. "I don't want any food," he said. "I am looking after myself. I am preparing for an operation."

Eccentric behaviour indeed, but the hotel staff dutifully acquiesced until the Friday evening when the manager entered the bedroom and found Delves Broughton in a coma. It transpired he had injected himself with fourteen shots of medinal and though rushed to the Northern Hospital he died at 2.25 on the Saturday morning. Cremation followed in Liverpool three days later and, on the following day, his ashes were laid to rest in the family vault at Broughton St Peter's Church, near Eccleshall. The mourners included Lady Vera, her daughter Lady Lovat and many tenants and employees from the estate. A memorial service was held later at the little church of St John's in the grounds of Doddington Hall.

At an adjourned inquest the principal witness was Delves Broughton's solicitor of six years, John Rothwell Dyson, of

Knightsbridge, London, who stated he had received two letters from his client, the first with a Latin quotation... "Moriturus te saluto" – I about to die salute thee. The second letter, "Not to be opened until after his death", contained confidential instructions which the coroner ruled private, "None of our business", although, of course, this was to add to further speculation that something earth-shattering had been revealed about Diana and Erroll's murder. After Delves Broughton had pledged to get her in the end!

He did not leave a suicide note, or any form of public explanation and, consequently, the jury returned the standard "suicide whilst the balance of his mind was disturbed", a relief to the family as, at that time, suicide without the "balance of mind" rider was deemed a criminal act and there would, most certainly, have been repercussions from any other verdict, especially regarding life insurance, if any existed.

The coroner obviously had a different opinion concerning Delves Broughton's state of mind, remarking prior to the jury's verdict, that in the accepted sense he had been fully in possession of all his faculties and there was no evidence he was of unsound mind.

Twelve Delves Broughton baronets are interred in the family vault at St Peter's Church.

Indeed there wasn't. On the contrary, he seems to have been perfectly sane when he wrote his "Moriturus te saluto" letter to his solicitor, or when he completed the formalities of his will in Nantwich before boarding a train to Liverpool. That said, given what he had gone through, it was hardly surprising he took his own life, and yet even this has been twisted by a number of writers and scurrilous wagging tongues who say it was an admission of his guilt, that he had, indeed, murdered Joss Erroll. Mind you, there's always an alternative theory and some believe Delves Broughton was actually bumped off by state spooks to prevent him from revealing the truth behind Erroll's murder.

Far more plausible is revenge and it was uppermost in Delves Broughton's mind when he hastily made his will in Nantwich, for had he died intestate, or had there been an earlier will, then his legal wife, Diana, would probably have copped for his entire personal estate, the value of which amounted to £8,334, a large amount in its day but a pale shadow of what his own father had left him.

The Great Gatsby had almost blown the lot and his will certainly made a mockery of Diana's £5,000-a-year pre-nuptial agreement. The Doddington estate, or what was left of it, was entailed in trust for his son and he had named Lady Vera as sole executor and in that capacity she made damned sure Diana didn't get a proverbial brass farthing.

St John's Church in Doddington Park.

17
Suspects and Motive

SO who did murder Lord Erroll? Dozens have claimed to know the "real story", but the problem has always been too many suspects with too many motives. Maybe it was Jock Delves Broughton, maybe it was a jilted lover, a vengeful husband or even a state-sponsored assassin. Or maybe not. Controversy, revisions, re-examinations and new theories, in print and on film, continue to fascinate and cloud the case, each raising multiple doubts and contradictory legends to leave Erroll's death in the pantheon of classic unsolved murders.

Take Gwladys Lady Delamere, the imperious Mayor of Nairobi, Happy Valley's chief muckraker, the Czarina of Nairobi's social life. Was she the killer, or did she have a hand in engineering the deed? Opinions certainly differ. Some say she was incensed that Erroll had refused to marry her and that she lied in court to cover up their relationship. She may also have been furious enough to write the Muthaiga Club taunting notes, but that did not make her a murderer, and, in any case, she had a sound alibi. To be Mayor of anywhere, of course, one has to be politically savvy and the object of the notes, her hidden agenda, may have been to work Delves Broughton into such a state of simmering rage that he would up-sticks and leave Kenya with his common tart in tow. It didn't work out that way and her hostility at the trial and afterwards was apparent for all to see.

But what about the basket case Alice? Trigger-happy, tempestuous Alice who had shot Raymond de Trafford in Paris, so coining the Muthaiga Club quip: "Where did she shoot him? The Gare du Nord? No, in the balls." A drug addict, suicidal and mentally unstable, Alice de Trafford had been a two-decades' notch on Erroll's bed-

Alice de Trafford,
a dubious alibi.

post and the story goes, widely known to still carry a candle for him, unhinged and consumed by jealousy, she flagged down Happy Valley's rampant Casanova and killed him – if she couldn't have him, nobody else would. Eight months later Alice shot herself in the heart and, apparently, left behind letters the Kenyan coroner censored because of what he considered to be "damaging revelations of a social and political nature". Maybe she had confessed, but who knows? Just as with Delves Broughton's inquest, the power of coroners was omnipotent and everyone else was left to second guess.

What seems odd, if Alice was the murderer, is why she chose to confront Erroll in the wartime blackout and in the middle of nowhere? How could she have known what time he would be driving past and how, single-handedly, had she managed to push a body weighing sixteen stones from the driving seat into the footwell of the Buick? The fundamental question also remains unanswered: Why murder Erroll – why not her love rival Diana?

Certainly until one of her lovers provided a dubious alibi, Alice was very much in the frame and, for a while, the police and the Nairobi colonials considered her the principal woman suspect, a view that filtered back after the war to Cheshire and the Tarporley Hunt Club, home turf of a string of aristocrats, members past and present, associated with Kenya.

Whatever was discussed over dinner in the Hunt Room at Tarporley's Swan Hotel, the wagons circled around the late Jock Delves Broughton, one of their own, and the only member in the club's long and illustrious history to stand trial on a murder charge. Years later, whilst researching the hunt club's past, secretary Gordon Fergusson claimed to have stumbled on information that, once and for all, cleared up the Erroll mystery and, in his book *Green Collars,* he unerringly named Alice de Trafford. This was picked up and commented on by the *Daily Telegraph's* Peterborough column: "Fresh claims are being made about the long-running White Mischief saga. In *Green Collars* Captain Gordon Fergusson claims to disclose the identity of Lord Erroll's murderer. He fingers Alice de Trafford. Fergusson enters the crowded field speaking of Mrs de Trafford's suicide note – an impeccable source."

Peterborough was not convinced and nor were members of the de Trafford family and, to be truthful, Fergusson did rather gild the

Cheshire's House of Lords, the Tarporley Hunt Club.

lily. His "impeccable source" turns out to have been the daughter of Alice's doctor who, when she was eleven-years-old, was told about the contents of Alice's letters. Still, throughout the rest of his life Fergusson asserted with confident authority that Alice was, indeed, the killer. "She had the motive, means and mentality," he maintained.

It was a further twist in the Erroll case, an enigma mulled over and scrutinised almost to saturation point by a posse of biographers, amateur sleuths and conspiracists. Everybody enjoys a rollicking good conspiracy and in *The Life and Death of Lord Erroll* the author, with questionable corroborating proof, claims there was an elaborate political assassination carried out by a Britain's Special Operations Executive (SOE) acting on the personal orders of none other than Prime Minister Winston Churchill. The case against Delves Broughton was concocted to cover up the real reason for Erroll's murder, i.e. his Fascist sympathies and involvement with a renegade group seeking appeasement with Hitler. Members of the group included the Duke of Windsor, Duke of Hamilton, Rudolph Hess and even Lady Vera Delves Broughton's Lord Moyne who, like Erroll, was also assassinated.

Admittedly a good yarn and an excellent read, added to by the fact that Erroll's first wife Lady Idina was sister-in-law to the head of MI6, there are a number of inconsistencies, not least the timings at odds with the facts and why didn't Britain simply order Erroll back to London and arraign him for treason? If he did have secrets these would easily have been suppressed by wartime censorship.

Then in another tome we have "conclusive proof" that Delves Broughton and Diana were actually secret agents sent to Kenya to kill Erroll. Vividly imaginative this one would do justice to Ian Fleming, "From Kenya with Love" with Delves Broughton cast as an unlikely 007. That said, there is an intriguing reference in a

Nantwich local newspaper from the summer of 1940: "Due to war work Sir Henry Delves Broughton had declined the honour of being appointed Cheshire's High Sheriff."

War work? He had been out of the army for twenty years, so to what was he alluding, or was it merely a blind to cover chronic money problems and his unpatriotic elopement with Diana?

Further supposition, first raised in the British press in the immediate aftermath of Erroll's death, was assassination by Nazi agents, the rationale being that his demise was expected to critically hamper Britain's East Africa campaign. However the majority of authors and investigators believe Delves Broughton was the murderer, a view endorsed by the discovery, many years later, of sensational tape recordings, "New evidence from beyond the grave".

The thrust of this one is premeditated murder, that Delves Broughton arranged an accomplice to collect him from the lonely road junction where he dumped Erroll's Buick. The accomplice is named as a neighbour, Dr Athan Philip, an ear, nose and throat specialist, who having fallen on hard times was happy to take a generous payment for doing the pick-up.

Finally, another author suggests Delves Broughton engaged his chauffeur as a hit-man to eliminate the leaping lord. Is it any wonder the murderer's identity has confounded and divided opinion for generations?

18

Here's to myself and one other !

THE intrigue still burns eighty years later and hardly a scrap of information has not been pored over. One who knew more than most about the crazy goings-on was schoolgirl Juanita Carberry, whose father and stepmother were very much part of the in-crowd, and in her book *Child of Happy Valley*, published in 1999, she provides a fascinating insight into what life was like: "Beneath the froth of the dancing, drinking, the overt liaisons, there lurked the element of the frantic. Many became addicts, either of drink or drugs."

This was the playground of Joss Erroll and the Carberrys and Juanita maintained she carried Jock Delves Broughton's secret for almost sixty years. Three days after the murder he had told her: "By the way, Juanita, I don't want you to be afraid, but the police are following me."

When she asked why, he said it was because they thought he had murdered Joss Erroll. "Well actually I did," he added. He then proceeded to tell her how he had done it – by hiding in the car. Juanita Carberry also revealed details of a haunting verse he scribbled in her autograph album which he signed and dated January 27, 1941:

Here's to myself and one other
And may that one other be she
Who drinks to herself and one other
And may that one other be me.

According to Juanita, a further conversation was abruptly halted by the appearance of Diana: "As soon as she saw Broughton she flew at him like a wildcat, punching and clawing at him, and screaming that he had killed Erroll. It was awful. Like most children I loathed rows and I fled. I never saw Broughton again."

Because she was perceived too young and unreliable, Juanita Carberry was not called as a trial witness, but her account is astonishing and, at face value, undeniably suggests Delves Broughton was, indeed, the murderer, although the obvious question is why a normally aloof English baronet would unburden himself and confess murder to a fifteen-year-old schoolgirl?

Juanita, perhaps rather naively, believed it was because she was a kindred spirit, a fellow outsider. Delves Broughton on the other hand was an experienced rider to hounds who knew all there was to know about false trails and this became evident when he eventually returned to Cheshire, bragging that he had paid an African man £1,000 to kill Erroll, whilst to another acquaintance he claimed to have personally pulled the trigger – "I've never run so fast in my life," he boasted as if trying to live up to his own notoriety, i.e. the infamous wife-seducer Erroll had got his just desserts and he'd had the guts to do it. One thing that may be said for certain is that he hadn't lost his knack of twisting the truth, whatever it was, into a Gordian knot.

When the police homed in on him as the prime suspect they built their case around two of the most powerful motives known to the human race, jealousy and revenge. But how jealous was he? Infatuated, besotted, yes, but for eight or nine years he'd been in a strange relationship with Diana, savouring the crumbs as she bedded a string of lovers, from her first husband Vernon Motion to Joss Erroll, and hadn't she cavorted with fellow ship passengers whilst he casually played bridge? Would it have been absurdly naïve to have expected her to suddenly become a faithful wife? Then there was the marriage pact and who is to say his acceptance of her partying and dancing was not part of their deal?

Delves Broughton's barrister and solicitor certainly believed that of all the cuckolded husbands propping up the public bars of Nairobi, he was the least likely to have murdered Erroll. However over those same public bars the mystery continued a topic of conversation for decades as it wasn't every day an eleventh baronet was accused of murdering a twenty-second earl who had stolen his wife when they were still practically on their honeymoon.

Perhaps, just perhaps, Delves Broughton did intricately plot and get away with a very clever murder, but if so, how did he pull it off? Surely not by shinning down a drainpipe, shooting Erroll and then returning to his bed, without Diana, June Carberry or the servants hearing him. As to his dash through the Bush this was ridiculously far-fetched and years after the trial the notion was dispelled, once and for all, by a rookie Kenyan police officer who went on to attain the rank of superintendent. Intrigued by the notorious murder he set off to test Delves Broughton's dead-of-night route from the lonely crossroads to the house at Karen. He didn't get very far on account of prowling lions!

In the end the Crown failed to prove beyond reasonable doubt that Delves Broughton had done the dastardly deed and as the Attorney General who presided at the trial said afterwards: "Whoever murdered Lord Erroll, Broughton was innocent by law – having been found not guilty by the jury after a fair trial."

There was never any real evidence to convict him and yet the rumours rumble on to this day that he was wrongly acquitted and throughout much of his own lifetime Sir Evelyn, Delves Broughton's son and heir, tried to defend his late father, notably in early 1987 when he challenged a finger-pointing article published in a Sunday

Charles Dance and Greta Scacchi
as Lord Erroll and Diana.

newspaper. His father, he said, had been put to bed drunk and, although he could hardly walk, the police maintained he had run across country in the middle of the night. It was absurd and although predicting the truth would one day come out, Sir Evelyn took care not to identify the killer, presumably because it just might have been perceived as libellous. Six months later, coincidentally just at the time the *White Mischief* film was being released, Diana died, the last of the principals involved in Erroll's murder.

Having waited a long time Sir Evelyn went on the offensive and named her as the likely murderer: "She was the thwarted lover because neither she nor Erroll had any money and he was never going to marry her without money. I am quite sure my father was not implicated in the murder in any way. He only married Diana because he was lonely and wanted companionship. It would not have been in his character to get upset just because she took a lover."

As to the blockbuster film which has since been watched by millions across the world, Sir Evelyn complained: "I was not consulted in any way. You can't libel a dead man, so they can say anything." The film's version of events was manifestly wrong as his father had been too drunk, old and infirm to have committed the crime. Unfortunately for his family honour the mud continued to stick and it still does, principally due to the film in which rumour and innuendo have been cleverly transformed into cast-iron fact to leave audiences convinced of Delves Broughton's guilt and that his acquittal was a shocking travesty.

Following Sir Evelyn's death, in 1993, his wife, equally incensed, took up the cudgel and submitted a stinging rebuke to the *Spectator* magazine for repeating that her father-in-law had got away with murder. Attacking James Fox's *White Mischief* book she insisted it would not have been written if Delves Broughton's revealing papers had been taken into consideration. Diana, she said, had been a gun-slinging nymphomaniac who'd had a passionate affair with an Italian, taken a lover on the ship to Africa and then asked another man to join them on their honeymoon. Delves Broughton's letters showed that once married he had despised her.

Sir Evelyn's and his wife's pleadings made no difference whatsoever. Most books, press articles, numerous television documentaries and, particularly the film, have posthumously crucified Jock Delves Broughton.

19

Everyone knows I did it

SO many have had a stab at solving Lord Erroll's murder and Delves Broughton's trial is the central plank, the furnace upon which practically every book has been forged. However one work that tends to deviate from the mainstream is Leda Farrant's *Diana, Lady Delamere* posthumously published in East Africa in 1997. Farrant spent the last years of her life researching the evidence and interviewing scores of people, including jurors, court witnesses, lawyers, relatives and the present Lord and Lady Delamere. Not one of them believed Delves Broughton was guilty and nor did the Nairobi-based *Sunday Nation* when, on the 25th anniversary of Erroll's death, it unerringly identified Diana as the murderer.

What followed was extraordinary. The allegation appeared only in the newspaper's early edition before being pulled and dropped altogether for fear of libel. A week or two later the *Nation's* managing director happened to be playing bridge at the Muthaiga Club and, finding himself at the same table as none other than Diana, he offered a stumbling, embarrassing apology. Brushing him aside and leaving others to speculate whether it was a confession or tongue-in-cheek, she responded cryptically – "Oh! Everyone knows I did it." As the author Leda Farrant put it, Diana always felt the truth was too precious to be cast like pearls before swine.

Interest in the mystery has never waned and with Diana's death and the *White Mischief* film captivating cinemagoers another newspaper, the *Sunday Independent* of Ireland, entered the fray by dispatching a journalist to Kenya to discover what was being said in Nairobi: "The talk in the Muthaiga Club is that Diana did it. She was beautiful, decadent and amoral. Oh yes, they'll tell you at the Muthaiga that Diana did it. Her husband (Delves Broughton) was never much liked – a boastful man who mistreated the natives – but he'd never have killed his own kind. In the stillness that surrounds this exclusive watering hole the spectre of Diana just will not go away."

So what did take place following the bizarre toast at the Muthaiga Club on that fateful early morning of January 24, 1941? Without attempting the herculean task of dissecting every morsel of evidence it is sufficient to say the housekeeper, Dorothy Wilks, claimed to have witnessed Erroll and Diana having a blazing row when they arrived at Karen House. Was this the catalyst for what was to follow?

Wilks stated there was a knock at the door and when she opened it Diana almost fell into the room with a face like thunder: "Lord Erroll was with her. It was obvious there had been a fight. There was none of the usual lovey-dovey stuff between them."

Was Erroll, the career seducer, dumping Diana, extricating from an affair that had gone way beyond one of his casual love 'em and leave 'em conquests? Given the trail of paramours in his wake it was probably an inevitable outcome. They had known each other barely two months and already Diana was seeing herself as the next Lady Erroll, Baroness Kilmarnock, but why would he want to marry a penniless divorcee with expensive tastes? He could dally with whom he pleased and they would always be grateful for the attentions of the great Lord Erroll. What he needed to sustain his glamorous lifestyle was another Idina or Molly, a wife with bags of money, and for all her undoubted allure Diana was not in that league, especially if Delves Broughton was steadfastly refusing to honour the £5,000-a-year prenuptial pact.

For what it's worth in a blizzard of whodunnit opinions the following is my personal theory, the circumstances loosely touched on in a television documentary presented by Oscar winning screenwriter Julian Fellowes who concluded that Diana was certainly present when Erroll was murdered:

- Karen House: Diana grabs her revolver, follows Erroll to his car and in a paroxysm of rage shoots him at point-blank range. She will go on to shoot at three future lovers, one of them surviving a near fatal bullet when he tries to end an affair.

- With Erroll's body slumped in the Buick she flees indoors and a native servant sees her tearing off a blood-spattered dress as she rushes up the stairs. The servant, like the housekeeper Wilks, is not called as a trial witness – Wilks because she has a crush on Delves Broughton and is considered biased, the servant simply because she is native.

- Panic-stricken Diana alerts Delves Broughton and June Carberry and their collective instinct is to move the body and the car away from Karen House as quickly as possible. Delves Broughton, English old school, feels honour-bound to protect his wife, no matter what, whilst June Carberry's stoic loyalty for her lesbian lover is beyond question.

- To conceal the evidence they drive two cars to the road junction, the Buick and, to return them to the house, either Carberry's or Delves Broughton's car.

• Their greatest difficulty is forcing Erroll's body into the Buick's central footwell to allow one of them to squeeze into the driver's seat. In their favour the gear lever is mounted on the steering column and they are not travelling very far.

• At the junction, well away from Karen House, they manouevre the Buick into the pit, leaving on the headlights to make it appear to have been an accident, although in their haste they turn off the ignition.

• Back at Karen House they concoct a story, a pack of lies, and initially the police don't make much of them. Delves Broughton states he was in a drunken sleep, Diana swears she didn't hear anything after Erroll's departure, and Carberry comes up with timings so precise they fuddle the investigation.

• On the morning of Erroll's death, too distraught and inconsolable to be interviewed by the police, Diana jumps into a car with June Carberry and rushes to Erroll's bungalow where, on the previous night, she had apparently demanded he burn her love letters. He'd refused and she was hell-bent on retrieving them. A vital piece of evidence apparently unknown to the police.

• Juanita Carberry, an impressionable teenager, witnesses Diana, like a wildcat, screaming at Delves Broughton that he'd killed Erroll. Could it have all been cleverly stage-managed?

• Delves Broughton and Diana go off on an eight-day hunting safari. When they return he is arrested and, whilst imprisoned awaiting trial, Diana and June Carberry visit him daily.

• Diana flies to South Africa to charm Harry Morris, the best in the business, into defending Delves Broughton, i.e. the man accused of murdering her one great love.

• At the trial Delves Broughton, an experienced magistrate familiar with the vagaries of circumstantial evidence, sashays with consummate ease around most everything the Crown throws at him.

• June Carberry is not so sure of herself when a member of the jury asks if she had in any way been an accessory, before or after the crime, or in the concealment of anybody of anything, "No, certainly not," she replies.

• Diana does not need to perjure herself as she is protected by spousal privilege from giving evidence in court.

• After the "Not Guilty" verdict Delves Broughton and Diana holiday together in Ceylon and India.

Such a strange sequence of events certainly suggests that Diana, Delves Broughton and June Carberry were the only ones who really knew the truth, and their pact, their togetherness, successfully saw off an appallingly cack-handed police investigation whose litany of mistakes included failure to examine the gun Diana always carried; failure to examine the cars belonging to June Carberry and Delves Broughton; failure to examine Diana's clothes, especially as the blood-stained hairgrip found in the Buick indicated a woman's involvement and, of course, the last known person to see Erroll alive was Diana.

In the end only Delves Broughton ever stood trial for the murder and, though acquitted, most writers have consistently tried to turn justice on its head to show otherwise. Perhaps they should have taken heed of his solicitor, Lazrus Kaplin, who always claimed he knew very well who had shot Lord Erroll. However his "lips were sealed", he said, until all the principals in the case were dead. His lips remained sealed. The only one to outlive him was Diana.

Enigmatic to the last, Diana took her secret to the grave.

20
The closing years

THIRTY-ONE and born with the century, Thomas Pitt Hamilton Cholmondeley became the 4th Baron Delamere at the beginning of one of the Britain's most tumultuous decades. Known as Tom Delamere, he was the first of his kin for sixty years to plant roots at Vale Royal following marriage in 1924 to Phyllis Anne Montagu Douglas Scott, a long-legged, breathtakingly beautiful aristocrat from the upper reaches of nobility. Descended on the male side from the Duke of Monmouth and King Charles II, her grandfathers were the 6th Duke of Rutland and Scotland's largest landowner, the 6th Duke of Buccleuch. Her uncle was Lord Francis Scott who stood as best man when Tom's father, the 3rd Lord Delamere, married Lady Gwladys Markham. Her cousins included the wife of the Duke of Gloucester, Princess Alice, and Lady Elmhurst, grandmother to present day Sarah, Duchess of York.

During his childhood Tom spent only brief periods at Vale Royal before it was rented out by his father's creditors to a prominent Manchester businessman, Robert Dempster, who had made a fortune from gas engineering. With his wealth and enthusiasm, Dempster proved a model tenant able to maintain at least some of Vale Royal's social prestige. He was exceedingly proud of its place in history and during his tenure of seventeen years he retained a staff of forty domestic servants and gardeners, and plenty there was to keep them occupied. Internally there were eighty-six rooms including the great hall, dozens of bedrooms, library, boudoirs, morning room, dining room, trophy room, armoury and Chinese room, some littered with relics from the former monastery, others with the few

Phyllis, a glamorous aristocrat. When she became Lady Delamere she frequently appeared in national magazine advertisements endorsing Pond's Face Powder.

Phyllis became the sixth Lady Delamere when she married Tom, the 4th Baron, in 1924.

works of art and lesser treasures that had escaped the 3rd Baron's purge. Outdoors the formal gardens, parkland, conservatories, coach-house and stables added to the richness of the setting, although by the First World War, and in spite of Dempster's deep pockets, Vale Royal was, like so many great houses of that era, an anachronism, just about clinging on to the halcyon days of the mid-19th century. The interior furniture and fittings, the décor and the rudiments of heating, lighting and plumbing had barely changed according to an eloquent and evocative account penned years later by Dempster's granddaughter who spent most of her young life at the rambling pile of antiquity:

Phyllis Lady Delamere.

Beside the house, like a large map, lay the foundations of the Abbey church which my grandfather excavated and laid out. When he went there nothing was visible above ground except a stone shrine known erroneously as the Nun's Grave. When the plan of the church was uncovered the shrine was found to mark the site of the high altar. My grandfather found the stone coffins of the monks lying around and these he filled rather incongruously with geraniums. The main reception rooms were on the first floor and the front door had originally been upstairs at the top of a flight of steps. The armoury led into the former monks' dortour, known as the Saloon. Immensely long it had huge Georgian windows into which were set off panes of ancient glass. The two large bay windows had the most fascinating curtains I've ever seen, the work of the first Lady Delamere. They were of velvet lavishly embroidered with gold thread and padded appliqué, and the motifs – coats of arms and great, fat Tudor roses as big as plates – were embossed in padded satin about two inches thick. There was a cabinet of historic relics and treasures but as few were labelled we had no idea what they were. Among them was a crystal replica of the Pitt diamond. The rooms known as the Skin Rooms housed Lord Delamere's collection of stuffed animals from Kenya. We regarded the lions, tigers and leopards in the glass cases as personal friends. An elephant's head fixed to the wall was so heavy that the iron staple that held it went through to the outside. The Skin Rooms had a strange smell of furs and mothballs and as they were fitted – as was the rest of the house – with acetylene gas, were very eerie at dusk or when one visited them at night with a candle. The dining room occupied the whole of the south-west wing. It contained two full-length portraits of Charles II

Vale Royal's Great Hall (Saloon) adorned with ancestral shields and coronets.

and James II and a Van Dyck, dated 1657, of Catherine, Viscountess Cholmondeley, wearing a necklace of pearls as big as cherries. There was another fine portrait of Lady Mary Cholmondeley, the 'Bolde Layde of Cheshire'. There were twenty-four identical beige leather dining chairs stamped with the letter D surmounted by a coronet in gold; and above the table hung a solid silver chandelier about five feet high and four feet wide which two footman on ladders had to clean every day. The principal bedrooms were in little suites. Most had enormous Victorian beds with draped testers. The third-best suite, known as the Oak Rooms, was panelled with black oak. Some of the panels were inscribed to record various royal visits and contained several large, ancient pictures, mostly black with age. One hanging above the wash stand, so I cleaned my teeth in front of it every day,

> depicted two almost identical Tudor ladies in ruffs, sitting side by side in bed, holding identical papooses in swaddling bands. The inscription recorded that the mothers were twins, married the same day and their infants born the same day. The picture is now in the Tate Gallery. There was always a heavy kind of silence pressing down on these rooms – so silent that it was almost sonorous with dim sounds from the past – and sometimes a loud crack would issue from one of the grotesquely carved chests or wardrobes. I always felt very creepy at night and was terrified to light the candle – let alone get out of bed in the dark.

The last of the Dempsters to live at Vale Royal was Robert's daughter Edith, a middle-aged spinster who inherited half her father's fortune before walking down the aisle of Whitegate Church to marry her suitor of two decades, Colonel Frank Pretty, of Ipswich. They soon left Vale Royal and moved to Suffolk where Edith was to become the driving force behind the discovery of the Sutton Hoo medieval hoard, one of the great archaeological finds of the 20th century.

In her younger days she had been inspired by excavations to establish the foundations of Vale Royal Abbey and on her estate at Sutton Hoo she teamed up with her odd-job man to investigate two mysterious mounds. Using jugs, bowls and sieves from the pantry, pastry brushes from the kitchen and bellows from the library they were soon uncovering the indentations of a long-vanished Viking ship. It turned out to be the largest haul of treasure ever recovered in Britain – jewels, coins, gold and silver plate, armour, weapons and decorative objects of every sort, and from as far away as Egypt and Byzantium. Edith ensured the treasure went to the British Museum, the single most valuable donation ever made by a living person.

Phyllis Lady Delamere with the children at Vale Royal in the 1930s.

Following the Dempsters, Tom and Phyllis Delamere took up residence at Vale Royal and, though they tried valiantly to preserve the extravagant entertainment and local munificence of their predecessors, the place was in sad decline and they were fighting a losing battle, especially as Tom's father, Lord Delamere, wanted rid of the lot, arguing it was more profitable to own property in Kenya rather than in England. As a consequence the 1928 estate sale occurred in order to ward off the receivers and the house with its immediate grounds was again rented out, this time to the Rimmers, an American family, who remained in occupancy until 1935 when Tom, by now the 4th Baron Delamere, returned with his wife and their three children, Elizabeth Florence Marion, Jeannetta Essex, and Hugh George. Tom and Phyllis's close friends were the Delves Broughtons, of Doddington Hall, and at the christening of Hugh

George, the would-be 5th Baron, Jock Delves Broughton was one of the godparents. Seven years later he would stand trial for murder in Kenya.

Tom in Welsh Guards' uniform.

At last back where he felt he belonged, Tom Delamere's homecoming coincided with the banks closing in on his late father's massive debts and, as he tried to salvage what little remained of his inheritance, he made a further attempt to reinstate Vale Royal to its rightful position at the top table of local society. A Cheshire Hunt Ball for three-hundred guests, in the finest traditions of Vale Royal, marked the zenith of his efforts, but sadly the omens were not good. And, as if to confirm the uncertainty, a Romney portrait inexplicably crashed to the floor, a sure sign in family legend that the days of the Delameres at Vale Royal were numbered.

Lady Phyllis with her daughters.

And so it came to pass. Faced with a mountain of debts, death duties, the outbreak of war and the house to be used as a sanatorium, Tom set out to dispose of Vale Royal's last treasures, including six valuable works of art which he sold through Christies of London. One of these, an enigmatic painting from 1600, was titled "The

Cholmondeley Ladies". It now hangs in the Tate Gallery.

Tom's marriage had been on the rocks for some time and when he rejoined his old regiment, the Welsh Guards, as a training adjutant, Phyllis moved away with the children. Four years later she was granted a divorce on the grounds of his adultery and for much of the rest of her life she lived in London. Tom, meanwhile, soon found himself the next Lady Delamere, Mary Ashley, the "enfant terrible" younger sister of Lord Louis Mountbatten's wife, Edwina, with whom she was joint-heiress to the £multi-million fortune of their late maternal grandfather, the international banking magnate Ernest Cassel.

A mother of two by first husband, Alec Cunningham-Reed, Mary's glitzy lifestyle frequently made front page news and she was quite a celebrity when, in 1943, Tom Delamere caught her on the rebound from two failed marriages. After the war they took up residence at Six Mile Bottom Hall, her family's large country estate on the edge of Newmarket, the perfect setting for Tom who was a fanatical racehorse owner and breeder. In business he formed a London-based advertising agency, Everetts, one of the acorns from which has grown the 21st century global communications conglomerate Saatchi and Saatchi.

Vale Royal was abandoned, its fate uncertain, as Tom began selecting faithful retainers, domestic servants and gardeners, to transfer to Six Mile Bottom Hall. The end came when he agreed to sell the ancestral home, lock, stock and barrel, to Cheshire County Council for use as a county police headquarters. The furniture remnants and the last of the books were sold through Brown's of Chester and, afterwards, hundreds of people turned up in Whitegate to bag an auction bargain, be it a chamber pot or a suit of armour. It was a humiliating, undignified end to eight generations of the family at Vale Royal.

Mary Lady Delamere, sister to Lady Louis Mountbatten.

Six Mile Bottom Hall and Newmarket racing had its attractions but Tom Delamere's heart was at Soysambu and, to perpetuate his father's colonial dream, he settled with Mary in Kenya, the heady days of Happy Valley notoriety having long since drifted away on the tides of history. Joss Erroll's murder had seen to that.

Tom knew very little about farming, but cushioned by his wife's wealth and an enormous stroke of luck – soaring cattle prices – he was able to extricate his father's estate from receivership. It meant, after years of uncertainty, Soysambu became a happier place, many friends and family holidaying with Tom and Mary, including her sister Edwina and Lord Mountbatten, the last Viceroy of India and

Personal Aide-de-Camp to Queen Elizabeth.

Tom and Mary went on to enjoy ten years of marriage until they were hit by a whirlwind, Kenya's cause célèbre, Diana, who was determined to become the eighth Lady Delamere of Vale Royal. Citing her as co-respondent, Mary successfully sued for divorce and returned to Six Mile Bottom Hall from where she owned a string of top racehorses, all registered under the name "Mary Lady Delamere", a title she always took great delight in using.

Her death occurred in 1986. She was buried at St George's Church, Six Mile Bottom and left an estate of £1.25 million.

Mary attended the coronation of Queen Elizabeth in 1953. Her peeress robe was designed by Norman Hartnell.

21

White Queen of Africa

WHATEVER her faults, self-centred, vain, main-chancer, even murderer, Diana was the only one of all the principals associated with Erroll's death to rise from the ashes. She came to be known as the "White Queen of Africa", principally due to her fourth husband, Tom, the 4th Lord Delamere of Vale Royal, and before him the dour, reclusive millionaire Gilbert Colville whom she married with Jock Delves Broughton scarcely cold in his grave.

Colville indulged her obsession for jewels and couturier clothes, gave her diamond rings, pearls the size of pebbles, racehorses, and racehorse stables and, most of all, Joss Erroll's former home and lovenest, Oserian, the "kennel for a bitch" as Delves Broughton so sarcastically put it. Colville's wealth also bought her status at a time when most Nairobi socialites had turned their backs on her.

The elegant perfectionist Diana spent Colville's money like water, somewhere in the region of £30,000 a year, a vast sum in the late forties and fifties, but small beer to the beef baron who reckoned to have been tax assessed for £100,000 when, in fact, he owed the Inland Revenue three-quarters of a million.

It's an understatement to say Colville's marriage to Diana was strange. Supposedly homosexual and impotent, he turned a blind eye and openly encouraged her extra-marital affairs to such an extent that, desperate for an heir, he asked his estate manager to impregnate his wife for him. Diana miscarried and they adopted a daughter. Eventually, when another chapter and another husband beckoned for Diana, they agreed to divorce.

Husband three
Gilbert Colville.

Tom Delamere had been in her sights ever since he moved to Kenya to settle at Soysambu, although at first he intensely disliked her and pledged never to allow "that woman" to cross his threshold. But this was Diana, and Diana always got what she wanted. In 1955 she married Tom and fulfilled a warning she had made to his wife, Mary, that one day she would be the next Lady Delamere. In *The Life & Death of Lord Erroll*, Diana is rightly portrayed as "... a woman with a past that seemed to glow round her like a glittering animal that wishes to attract certain species and to repel others. One look from those steel-blue eyes could entrap and kill."

As pliant as ever, Gilbert Colville had agreed to an amicable divorce and for the rest of their lives the three of them remained great friends, Colville's money often bankrolling Tom and Diana who created an apartment for him at Soysambu. When he died in 1960, Colville left his estate to Diana who, to cover death duties, more or less sold the lot for a conservative estimate of £2.5 million. A Lady Delamere of Vale Royal had finally hit the jackpot.

During the 1950s and early 1960s, Tom became a pivotal and controversial figure in British resistance to Kenya's Mau Mau uprising and, at the height of simmering racial tension, he was at the forefront when settlers stormed the governor's residence. In 1964, just sixty years after Tom's parents took up land on the edge of the Rift Valley, the fully independent Republic of Kenya was created. Many settlers opted to leave rather than subject to African rule, but Tom

Tom Delamere, made Diana his third wife.

remained and acquired citizenship having been assured by Britain that he would retain his peerage as long as the country remained within the Commonwealth. Traces of colonial rule were not allowed to linger and, much to Tom's sorrow, his father's bronze statue in Nairobi, a striking symbol of colonialism, was removed and replaced by one of the country's first president, Jomo Kenyatta, whilst the main thoroughfare, Delamere Avenue, was renamed Kenyatta Avenue. Removal of the statue was a disservice to history, similar to the intolerant modern obsession for toppling monuments and memorials in order to erase and distort the past. Lord Delamere's statue was one of the first to succumb, but at least it was relocated to Soysambu and there it stands to this day, facing out towards a mountain known locally as "Delamere's Nose" or the "Sleeping Warrior".

Lord Delamere's statue shortly before it was removed from the centre of Nairobi.

To be fair, Diana proved to be a good wife to Tom in what must have been a mutually tolerant open marriage. In return he taught her to be a lady and soon they were very much a celebrity couple in Kenya. Soulmates, they shared a passion for foreign travel and horseracing, owning, breeding and training major winners in Kenya, including the Kenya St Leger, Derby and Gold Cup. Tom's colours were black with pink sash, sleeves and cap whilst Diana's were emerald green with scarlet sleeves and cap, and there was always an edge when they raced against each other. They also owned horses in England and, when not cruising together in the Mediterranean, they attended many of the principal race meetings in Europe. For all that, Diana's insatiable sexual appetite did not diminish and she continued with her assignations, still unpredictable and dangerous where her lovers were concerned.

It's said she and Tom lived in a ménage-à-trois for years at Soysambu with her lesbian lover, Lady Patricia Fairweather. As Hugh Cholmondeley, the 5th Baron Delamere, reflected on his step-

Nairobi Races 1969: Tom Delamere looks on as Diana receives the Uhuru Cup from President Jomo Kenyatta.

mother Diana: "She was the best whore in the country for fifty years. She liked men, would jump into bed with any woman that would have her, and she liked seducing gays."

Happy together: Diana and Tom Delamere.

Tom, 4th Baron Delamere, died in 1979 and Diana's idyll came to a close. She was sixty-six and took an apartment in London where she stayed for a few months each year, spending the rest of her time in Kenya. Eight years later she passed away, the former nightclub hostess, an enigma at the centre of the Erroll murder mystery. She had turned the international spotlight on the lifestyle of Happy Valley and as Lady Delamere of Vale Royal became the most powerful white woman in Africa.

Diana in her final days.

She is buried in the shade of a fig tree in a small hilltop cemetery she built on Gilbert Colville's ranch. Alongside her are the graves of Colville and Tom Delamere. The three inscriptions she wrote herself. For Colville: "If you want a memorial look around you". For Delamere: "So great a man". For herself: "Surrounded by all I love".

22

The wheel turns full circle

Doddington Hall in its heyday was one of Cheshire's finest country houses, a neo-classical masterpiece built to mark the union of the Delves and Broughton families. Designed by leading architect Samuel Wyatt, the grounds landscaped by Capability Brown, the magnificent hall was erected shortly before 1800 to replace a Jacobean house and 14th century castle, a fragment of which incongruously survives in Doddington Park, complete with stone embellishments of the Black Prince and his four Cheshire squires of Poitiers. Over the centuries more than a few eccentric Delves Broughtons have lived at Doddington Hall, none more so than its first occupant, the Rev. Sir Thomas Delves Broughton, a four times married father of thirteen children. In addition to the hall, cottages, stables and model farm the Reverend, probably to impress a prospective new wife, also commissioned the building of an elegant banqueting hall in the centre of Doddington Lake. Alas, the lady politely turned down his marriage proposal, stating she had fourteen reasons for doing so – herself and her own concerns was one reason, the other thirteen were his children from former marriages. The Reverend responded by blowing up the banqueting hall.

BRITISH Army officer Major Sir Evelyn Delves Broughton was certainly not thinking about ancestry when he opened his wartime mail in Baghdad a year after his father's death. Rather than comforting news from home, there was a terse note from his stepmother, Diana, enclosing a bill for £5,000, Harry Morris's defence fee, which she had no intention of paying. She had done her duty, engaged Morris and saved Jock from the gallows, and now it was Evelyn, the 12th Baronet Delves Broughton's problem.

Since the 1930s when she was a regular guest at Doddington, Evelyn had loathed and laughed at Diana, but who was laughing now? His father had gone to his grave leaving him debts and a tenth of the estate he might have expected to inherit. Now, with Morris's bill, courtesy of Diana, he was even deeper in the mire, especially as he had developed a taste of his own for the good life which was hardly surprising having grown up in the profligate shadow of his remote father who paid him little attention. In fact, during five years at Eton, Sir Jock only visited him once and James Fox's *White Mischief* book tells of Evelyn being allowed to attend race meetings at Epsom and often coming across his father in the grandstand.

At Eton, Evelyn escorts his mother, Lady Vera.

Evelyn went on to Cambridge and when he came of age he soon began to discover there was hardly anything left of his inheritance, though when he confronted his father he was chased out of his study with a riding crop. "Whatever there was in the kitty was practically bugger all," he said. "It was something like £50,000. All the money from the sale of the land was gone."

Five years later at the age of twenty-six, and in the midst of world war, Evelyn became, in name at least, the new master of Doddington, Samuel Wyatt's stately hall, Capability Brown's sweeping parkland, where General Dwight D. Eisenhower temporarily based his European headquarters and where units of the American army rigorously trained for the D-Day invasion. All around was an ugly sprawl of Nissen huts, pre-fabs, administrative buildings, communal wash-houses and toilet blocks, a military camp that until the late 1950s came to be used to house upwards of one thousand displaced Polish families.

With money tight and Doddington's future uncertain, Sir Evelyn, always enormously popular with his tenantry, returned from the war determined to convert what was left of the Delves

A daunting Doddington homecoming for Sir Evelyn.

Broughton estate into a profitable enterprise and, at the same time, repair some of his father's mind-boggling extravagance. It was a daunting task and his first action was to lease out the hall to a private girls' school, Goudhurst College, an establishment that was to remain for almost forty years.

Sir Evelyn marries pioneering Lord Delamere's granddaughter, Elizabeth Cholmondeley.

In 1947 the story of the Delameres and the Delves Broughtons turned full circle when Evelyn married the Hon. Elizabeth Cholmondeley, eldest daughter of Tom, the 4th Baron Delamere, and his first wife Phyllis. Two cash-strapped society families united, the wedding took place at St Margaret's Church, Westminster, and when six-hundred gathered for a sumptuous reception at Claridge's, impecuniousness was definitely not on the menu. The principal guests included Evelyn's mother Lady Vera, Tom Delamere's second wife Mary and her sister Viscountess Mountbatten.

The Delamere – Delves Broughton marriage was never a happy one and it ended in the divorce court. Afterwards the Hon. Elizabeth is said to have headed for Kenya to stay with her father, 4th Baron Tom, and his new wife, Diana, the latest Lady Delamere of Vale Royal. At Soysambu, Elizabeth apparently struck up a friendship with one of Diana's former lovers, Peter Leth, a big-game hunter and former commando noted for his "natural endowments" and keen eye for the ladies. Leth's previous dalliances with Diana had come to an abrupt climax when, echoes of Joss Erroll, he tried to end their relationship and she shot him! He survived and Gilbert Colville paid for his silence, although later, behind Tom Delamere's back, they resurrected their affair. Meanwhile, in Cheshire, Sir Evelyn went on to marry Helen Mary Shore who, at twenty-one, was Britain's youngest woman barrister. They had three daughters and a son and heir, John Evelyn Delves Broughton. Tragically, at the age of two, John died in a freak accident whilst the family was residing in a staff cottage on the Doddington estate. An inquest in Nantwich ruled the boy's death from asphyxiation had been a chance in a million accident brought on by falling into an ornamental pond.

The tragedy tore apart the Delves Broughton marriage, wife and husband blaming each other and both grieving for the loss of their son. Separation followed and they divorced in 1974, officially due to Sir Evelyn's unreasonable conduct. The judge made an order

Sir Evelyn with second wife Helen Mary and daughter Isabella.

for joint custody of the children with care and control to remain with Helen Mary.

Years later their eldest daughter, Isabella, vividly recalled having to shake hands with her mother on the day she walked out of her life. Isabella Delves Broughton, better known latterly as Izzy Blow, went on to carve a career as an iconic fashion guru with *Vogue* and the *Sunday Times*. Another to be afflicted by what seemed to have become a family curse, she committed suicide at the age of forty-eight after being diagnosed with ovarian cancer.

Sir Evelyn had troubles of his own following his third marriage, this time to Rona Crammond, a former pupil of Doddington's Goudhurst College. Similar to his father's relationship with very much younger Diana, Evelyn was fifty-nine, Rona thirty-four. A year into their marriage Evelyn was admitted into hospital for removal of a varicose vein, but when gangrene set in his leg had to be amputated. Disabled and in constant pain for the rest of his life he became almost wholly dependent on his much younger wife. When he died in 1993, the value of his properties had soared into the stratosphere over fifty years and he left just short of £4 million, most of it to Lady Rona, including his house in Kensington and the Doddington estate.

The presumed 13th Baronet is Sir Evelyn's cousin David Delves Broughton, though succession remains unproven and the title lies dormant. Lady Rona, a high-roller corporate investor and £multi-million "name" with Lloyd's of London, is planning to convert Doddington Hall into a five-star luxury spa hotel, financed through the building of one-hundred homes in Doddington Park.

23
Trigger Happy Valley

THE Delameres still farm at Soysambu, fifty thousand acres and one of the largest milk and livestock producing ranches in Kenya. Head of the family is Hugh, the 5th Lord Delamere, who lives with his wife Lady Anne in a sprawling bungalow overlooking Lake Elmenteita.

The daughter of Sir Patrick Renison, the last Governor of Kenya, Anne was introduced to Hugh by his now infamous stepmother, Diana. They have been married for over fifty years, most of their time leading a quiet life away from the controversy and notoriety that has raged ever since the 3rd Lord Delamere tore up his ancestral roots at Vale Royal and risked all to make a new life.

The Hon. Tom Cholmondeley
(1968 - 2016)

Sadly their lives were shattered in 2005 when their son, the 6th Lord Delamere in-waiting, the Honourable Thomas Patrick Gilbert Cholmondeley, shot and killed a native wildlife ranger, the repercussions of which transformed him into one of the most divisive and, ultimately, tragic figures in Kenya's brief history.

Expelled from Eton in the 1980s for wanton behaviour, Tom Cholmondeley, a towering man of 6ft-6ins, settled in Kenya where he was considered an outstanding farmer, conscientious and diligent, particularly in his attention to the quality of the land and soil. He was responsible for the design and layout of the Soysambu Wildlife Sanctuary and the building of Delamere Camp in 1993, a high-class lodge resort within a 6,000-acre sanctuary covering the area around Lake Elmenteita.

Tom Cholmondeley claimed the ranger's death had been a terrible accident and, from lack of evidence, he got away with it, much to the disgust of the majority who said it was due to class and position. On the one hand he was seen as a privileged, cravat-wearing white toff, a swaggering ex-public schoolboy with a fierce temper, whilst others closer to him maintained he was charming, a brilliant farmer and conservationist and an enlightened employer who had created hundreds of new jobs for local people and spoke to them in their own language.

At the root of it all was the tinderbox of Kenyan land ownership,

The Delamere dynasty. Tom Cholmondeley with his parents Hugh and Anne.

Cholmondeley determined to protect Soysambu from encroachment, indigenous Kenyans believing the land had been stolen from them in the first place by colonial settlers, especially his great grandfather, at the beginning of the 20th century.

Whatever the truth, Tom Cholmondeley escaped prosecution on a legal technicality, but within a year he had shot and killed a second man he discovered, with four others, poaching impala on the Soysambu estate. Cholmondeley maintained they were carrying machetes and bows and arrows and when he turned his gun on their dogs, a stray bullet accidentally hit the man who later died in hospital.

On this occasion there was no escape and charged with murder Cholmondeley faced the death penalty as he awaited trial, confined in a tiny cell in Nairobi's Kamiti maximum security prison, the only white man amongst 3,600 inmates. The world's press seized on the story and, resurrecting Joss Erroll's murder and the hedonistic lifestyle of the 1920/30s, photographs of a handcuffed Tom Cholmondeley appeared under the headline "Trigger Happy Valley".

Stoking up fierce resentment in Kenya, the affair then took on a macabre twist when Gwladys Lady Delamere's grave was desecrated and her skull was stolen from the family's private cemetery, an incident similar to an attack, years before, in which the skull of the 3rd Lord Delamere had also vanished.

In due course, the Honourable Thomas Cholmondeley was found guilty of the lesser charge of manslaughter and, finally, in 2009, he walked away a free man. Interviewed at the time he said: "I've been portrayed as this great monster who goes round shooting black men for sport when my whole life I've striven to move away from racist behaviour. The problem is I'm a very easy target. I'm a white man, toffee-nosed, titled and, on top of that, a white man in Africa."

Seven years later, and almost unbelievably, Cholmondeley, the scion of Kenya's most famous family, was dead after being admitted to a Nairobi hospital for hip replacement surgery following which he suffered cardiac arrest. Buried in a quiet corner of Soysambu ranch near the simple stone grave of his pioneering great-grandfather, he left two sons, Hugh and Henry, from a marriage that had ended in divorce in 2010. Hugh, born in 1998, is now the 5th Baron Delamere's heir apparent.

The family of the game warden shot by his father in 2005 told the *Kenyan Daily Nation* that Masai elders had conducted a ritual at the graveside of their relative to curse his killer. Their lawyer told the newspaper: "It was a serious thing and it was conducted by very elderly Masai. So when the elders heard the news of Cholmondeley's death they knew it was confirmation that their rituals still work."

In one way or another tragedy and scandal has dogged the privileged lifestyle of the Delamere clan in Kenya. Take Michael Cunningham-Reid, son of the 4th Baron Delamere's second wife, Mary Ashley. Following independence, Cunningham-Reid remained in Kenya and, in a further astonishing sequel in the *Loves and Lives of the Delameres*, his son-in-law, Antonio Trzebinski, was shot through the heart and killed two miles from the lonely crossroads where, sixty years before, Lord Erroll had been murdered.

Trzebinski, the husband of Cunningham-Reid's stepdaughter Anna, was eerily on his way to a rendevouz with his mistress. An international designer whose clientele includes Kate Moss, Princess Caroline of Monaco and Jemima Khan, Anna went on to marry a semi-nomadic tribal warrior and she now combines her time between her elegant house in a suburb of Nairobi, his rural village and the fashion shows of London and Paris.

THE LADY DELAMERES OF VALE ROYAL IN THE COUNTY OF CHESTER

1. 1821 - 1852 Henrietta Williams-Wynn, wife of Thomas Cholmondeley,1st Baron Delamere.

2. 1855 - 1859 Sarah Hay Drummond, 1st wife of Hugh Cholmondeley, 2nd Baron Delamere.

3. 1860 - 1887 Augusta Seymour, 2nd wife of Hugh Cholmondeley, 2nd Baron Delamere.

4. 1899 - 1914 Florence Anne Cole, 1st wife of Hugh Cholmondeley, 3rd Baron Delamere.

5. 1928 - 1931 Gwladys Markham, 2nd wife of Hugh Cholmondeley, 3rd Baron Delamere.

6. 1931 - 1944 Phyllis Anne Scott, 1st wife of Thomas Cholmondeley, 4th Baron Delamere.

7. 1944 - 1955 Ruth Mary Ashley, 2nd wife of Thomas Cholmondeley, 4th Baron Delamere.

8. 1955 - 1979 Diana Colville, 3rd wife of Thomas Cholmondeley, 4th Baron Delamere.

9. 1979 Anne Willoughby Renison, wife of Hugh Cholmondeley, 5th Baron Delamere.

Epilogue

FROM Lord Delamere's arrival at the beginning of the 20th century to the tragedy of his great-grandson Tom Cholmondeley in the early years of the 21st century, the name "Delamere" has been synonymous with controversy and discord in Kenya. The fact that pioneering Lord Delamere gave his all, his fortune and his life, for the country is relegated to an almost inconvenient footnote in history.

The family remains at Soysambu and. otherwise. the only tangible reference to the man himself, and well might he have smiled at the irony, is the sophisticated "Lord Delamere Terrace" at the upmarket Norfolk Hotel in Nairobi where once he turned the tables into a steeplechase course. Today it is internationally recognised as one of the greatest lounge bars in the world.

Lord Erroll's murder occurred a decade after Delamere's death and what turned it into a sensation was the enthralling 1987 film starring Charles Dance and Greta Scacchi as one of the most elegant, sexually charged couples in cinema history. Setting the scene for a myriad of books and documentaries to follow, *White Mischief* glamorised the ex-pat Happy Valley elite and paid scant attention to accuracy, notably in the climax portraying Jock Delves Broughton shooting himself in Kenya.

As to Vale Royal Abbey, it had a checkered history following Tom, the 4th Baron, and purchase by Cheshire County Council who, perhaps realising the enormity of the task, quickly off-loaded to Imperial Chemical Industries (ICI), initially as a hostel for Polish ex-servicemen workers. Later the company converted the eighty-six room former mansion into its Salt Division administrative headquarters but, by 1963, Vale Royal, empty and in a pitiful structural state, was being earmarked as a maximum security prison, a suggestion the local community uncompromisingly resisted.

Next it became the Vale Royal of England Club & Hotel as described by the Cheshire author Bob Westall: "They painted the Gothic vaulting of the cloisters an ice-lolly orange, daubed silly smirks on the faces of Gothic carvings and lit the whole with black iron Merrie England light-fittings."

Fortunately, the sacrilege was brief and Vale Royal was converted into a conference venue and training school for insurance salesmen, later an education centre for handicapped young people. Last in a long line of commercial optimists, a South African businessman purchased the demolition-threatened pile and proposed to turn it into sixteen apartments. The beginning of Vale Royal Abbey's renaissance finally commenced in 1995 when planning permission was granted to DHC (Bradford) Ltd to develop the former mansion and create a golf course and clubhouse, along with fifteen apartments and fifty executive homes. £1,889,000 exchanged hands and Vale Royal Abbey Golf Club opened for business in 1998.

It has taken almost one hundred and fifty years of decline to restore Vale Royal Abbey to its magnificent best and, just maybe, the ghosts and the "Lives and Loves of the Delameres" really are laid to rest, at least in Cheshire!

A new chapter in the thousand years history of Vale Royal. Below is 3rd Lord Delamere's simple grave at Soysambu.